The Odyssey of Tobacco

The Odyssey of Tobacco

BY ROBERT LEWIS FISHER

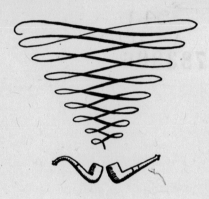

1939

THE PROSPECT PRESS

Litchfield, Connecticut

The Case, Lockwood & Brainard Company
Hartford, Connecticut 1939

TO

L. L. F.

Preface

WE TAKE SMOKING so much for granted today that few people give any thought to its past history. Even the most confirmed tobacco addict is apt to know but little of the origin of smoking or of how it came to be such a universal habit—yet the discovery of tobacco by what we are accustomed to call the civilized world and its subsequent spread to all parts of the earth resulted from momentous historical events. The custom of smoking and the tobacco plant itself went with the explorers and soldiers, the settlers and traders of the late sixteenth and early seventeenth centuries, so that in following the course of tobacco from one country to another one reads of the discovery and conquest, the colonization and development of a large part of the world.

In a little more than a century after the Europeans had first learned of tobacco through seeing the American Indians smoking, the habit had been introduced into almost every corner of the globe. The rapidity with which the practise spread from country to country is surprising, not only because of the difficulties of travel at the time, but also because of the many prohibitions of smoking—royal taboos which, by the severity of their enforcement, make our own late Eighteenth Amendment seem like an indulgent mother's "Junior, you shouldn't do that!" Few other social customs, and certainly no other mere plant, ever faced such widespread and determined opposition, and tobacco's eventual triumph over all obstacles rightfully entitles it to be called, as it is by one writer, "the hero among plants."

To trace the spread of smoking throughout the world is not an easy task. At times the available records are very meagre; at other times mistakes of early scholars have clouded what otherwise might have been a clear-cut story. By using both direct and indirect testimony we are finally able to reconstruct a reasonably accurate chronicle of the travels of tobacco around the globe, but our story must of necessity be based upon a mixture of fact and inference.

It is particularly disappointing to be unable to find full information about the introduction of smoking into some of the European nations which later became active propagators of the use of tobacco. We must, I think, expect to encounter this condition of uncertainty, if not of actual ignorance, when we study the sixteenth century's great maritime nations whose ships plowed restlessly across the Atlantic. So many of the sailors and soldiers and settlers who visited the New World became acquainted with the natives' use of tobacco that it is possible that many men of the same country may have brought the custom back to their homeland as, at one time and another, they returned from their western ventures. Furthermore, if these members of the vanguard of the great army of smokers were, as seems likely, just ordinary seamen, common soldiers and settlers of low degree, it is quite probable that their new pleasure was sometimes ignored by their very superior superiors, who, being the only literate people of the day, were the only ones who might have penned reports or reminiscences which would tell the story to us. We are lucky enough to have some accounts of that sort, but they are all too rare.

When the records as to just when some nation in its turn took up smoking are very scanty or confusing, we are sometimes able to uncover valuable circumstantial evidence. We frequently know the approximate time when the tobacco plant itself was first imported into a country, and, of course, the dates of many of the prohibitions of smoking are matters of actual record. From these known data we can make fairly acceptable deductions as to the time when different people began to smoke, if better testimony is not available.

For instance, it is safe to assume that (except in those European countries where tobacco was first grown merely because of its beauty or its medicinal properties) the active cultivation of the plant must have followed the rise of smoking by quite a few years; this appears logical, for presumably no farmer would undertake to raise a crop of tobacco until after he felt that there were enough smokers in his country to assure a satisfactory demand for his product. Likewise, a royal decree against the use of tobacco would hardly be promulgated until after the custom had become sufficiently popular and widespread to make a monarch feel constrained to save his subjects from becoming victims of what he considered to be a vicious habit. Therefore, it would seem sound, when lacking better evidence, to infer that the introduction of smoking into any given country took place ten years before the initial cultivation of the plant, and perhaps twice as long before the first edict banning the habit.

ix

I hope that the reader who is a devotee of the cigar or cigarette will not feel that this book places an undue emphasis on pipes. There are two reasons and two excuses for their prominence here. The first reason is that by and large the practice of smoking was carried from one country to another by pipe-smokers; the second is that pipes, being durable, provide us with valuable evidence of tobacco habits in past times and distant places, which such expendible smoking materials as cigars and cigarettes are, by their very nature, less capable of doing. The excuses are merely my own preference for pipes as the pleasantest means of taking tobacco, plus my personal interest in pipes of all years and of all countries as fascinating collectors' items.

I can make no claim of originality for this book. Whatever merit it may have lies in the fact that it is confined to a single phase of the history of tobacco—the spread of smoking throughout the world—and sets forth in one volume all the information on that subject which I have been able to glean from many different sources. That material is presented here not with the idea of providing a serious, technical work for historians, but with the hope that the reader of this small volume may be interested in and entertained by the story of the spreading of one of the pleasantest amenities of our present-day civilization.

R. L. F.

Litchfield, Connecticut
October, 1939

Table of Contents

List of Illustrations

The Odyssey of Tobacco

The Mayan Heritage

1

QUOTATIONS from early Greek and Roman philosophers and historians are generally supposed to give a book a becoming atmosphere of learning, so perhaps it would be proper to follow the usual pedantic style and begin this one by stating that the earliest authority on smoking was Herodotus, who wrote of Scythians who inhaled the fumes of some unidentified leaves thrown upon an open fire—and thereby became intoxicated to the point of stupefaction. That pedagogical vein could be continued by citations from present-day antiquarians who say that there are representations of smoking parties in some of the paintings found in tombs of the early Egyptian Pharaohs. But once we were started on that sort of thing, we would find that there is no end to the list of the various theories about the antiquity of smoking. There are, of course, some people who claim that smoking, like so many other attributes of our present-day civilization, was originated by the Chinese. Pleasant pictures are suggested by the archaeologists who maintain that the discovery of pipes in certain early Roman ruins on the site of Hadrian's Wall in the north of England proves that in the first century of our era Roman soldiers of the Sixth Legion comforted themselves with tobacco while guarding that northernmost outpost of the far-flung Roman Empire.

The theories just mentioned assuredly have some foundation of fact, as it is doubtless true that various people smoked in different ages of the distant past—but their kind of smoking had little or no connection with the habit as we know it today. It is almost certain, for instance, that those early smokers did not actually have tobacco, but used instead the dried leaves of sundry other herbs, plants, or trees. Furthermore, they evidently indulged in smoking either purely for its narcotic effect or else as a religious rite. In any event, it is impossible to ascribe our present habit to a development from any of these old customs, and, since this book should be pervaded by an aroma of tobacco rather than by an aura of erudition, it might be well to desert Herodotus and the rest of his ilk right now and start in with a more realistic approach to the history of the current social custom of tobacco-smoking purely for pleasure. This practise can be traced directly back to the Mayan race, which flourished in Central America and attained such a high degree of civilization in the first century, A.D.; beyond the Mayas we cannot go with any degree of assurance. Indeed, much of the history of the custom from the days of the early Mayas to more recent times is unknown, but this much is certain, that in 1492 the tobacco-smoking habit as practised by the Mayas was first discovered by Europeans, who in the next hundred years spread their new-found pleasure all around the world.

In these skeptical days, iconoclasm—or perhaps it is fairer to say better research—seems to have endowed most of our childhood heroes with clay feet. Just as we have been told that there is no Santa Claus and that Washington never threw a dollar across the Potomac, so have we heard that Watts did not invent the steam engine, nor Stephenson the locomotive, nor Fulton the steamboat. In fact, some people even say that the Wrights were not the first to invent a successful heavier-than-air flying machine and deny that Pershing ever said, "Lafayette, we are here."

Columbus was one of the heroes of our grammar school days because we had been taught that he discovered America. Later he was stripped of some of his glamour, when as high school or preparatory school students we heard that he had been preceded to the Western Hemisphere by more people than could be comfortably accommodated in the Yankee Stadium—a perfect legion of early "discoverers" who, historians believe, included Basques, Norsemen, Irishmen, Welshmen and Poles, as well as Buddhist priests, Egyptians, Romans, Arabians, Phoenicians, Scythians, and the inhabitants of the lost Atlantis—in fact, almost every known nationality except the Argentines and the Greeks. But even if Columbus is thus shorn of much of the glory with which we surrounded him in our childhood days, for those of us who grew up to be smokers he can always retain at least one undisputed and undivided claim to fame, for he led the expedition which first brought to the then civilized world the knowledge of smoking.

The discovery of tobacco-smoking by men of his company was described by Columbus in his own journal of his first voyage. That document, unfortunately, has been lost, but an abridged version of it was discovered and published about 1875, after having lain in manuscript form for more than three centuries. The abridgement is the work of Bartolomé Las Casas, who accompanied Columbus on his second voyage and who later became Bishop of the West Indies. From it we learn that after the Pinta, the Niña and the Santa Maria had first anchored at San Salvador, the voyagers cruised about among the other islands of the Antilles and arrived off the coast of Cuba on October 27, 1492. Columbus sent inland a party consisting of two of his own men and two natives who had accompanied him from the other islands, in order to explore the new island further and to search for the gold which he was confidently expecting to find; as he still believed, of course, that he had reached the Indies which were the original goal of his voyage, Columbus gave to the two Spaniards, Luis de Torres and Rodrigo de Jerez, letters of introduction to the Khan of Cathay. When the little expedition returned to the ships on November 5, 1492, the Spaniards had to report that, although they had visited many native villages and had been kindly received by the inhabitants, they had not succeeded either in discovering gold or in meeting the Khan of Cathay. They related that they had (to quote Las Casas)

    " . . . met with great multitudes of people, men and women, with firebrands in their hands and herbs to smoke after their custom."

Columbus had previously seen the same herbs in the possession of the Indians. He had written in his journal (at this point Las Casas quotes Columbus verbatim) as follows:

    "Monday, October 25th . . . Being at sea, about midway between Santa Maria and the large island, which I

4

name Fernandina, we met a man in a canoe going from Santa Maria to Fernandina; he had with him a piece of bread which the natives make, as big as one's fist, a calabash of water, a quantity of reddish earth, pulverized and afterwards kneaded up, and some dried leaves which are in high value among them, for a quantity of it was brought to me at San Salvador. . . ."

But none of the explorers knew the use which the Indians made of the dried leaves nor saw the actual practice of smoking until de Jerez and de Torres watched the natives of Cuba indulging in the habit, and even then the Spaniards did not have the slightest conception of the importance of their find. Just as Columbus was ignorant of the true nature of the lands which he had found, believing them to be the East Indies and not the New World, so did the discoverers of smoking fail to appreciate the significance of the strange Indian custom of which they had been the first European witnesses. There is no evidence that de Jerez and de Torres took any real interest in the peculiar practice of the aborigines of Cuba (despite some published statements that they were the first European smokers) nor that any of their companions or countrymen availed themselves of the pleasures of tobacco until several decades later.

The custom which de Jerez and de Torres had been the first white men to witness had been practised by the natives of the Western Hemisphere for many centuries. What is generally accepted as the oldest extant representation of tobacco-smoking is a bas-relief figure carved on a stone found in a Mayan temple at Palenque, in the present state of Chiapas, Mexico. The sculpture shows a Mayan priest, in ceremonial robes and elaborate head-dress, smoking a

5

straight, or tube, pipe, presumably as part of some religious rite. As the date of the temple is somewhere around one hundred years after the birth of Christ, it is evident that by that time the Mayas had learned to smoke, although perhaps only in connection with their religious rituals.

The history of smoking for the next fourteen hundred years is a closed book. We know only that in these centuries it became a common personal practice (although still retaining ceremonial characteristics in some instances) throughout all of Central America and the islands of the Caribbean Sea, through all of South America except the western coast and the extreme southern regions, and throughout what is now the United States and southeastern Canada. Early European explorers to all those parts of the Western Hemisphere found the natives smoking tobacco, and subsequent archaeological discoveries in those regions have uncovered a great deal of pre-Columbian smoking paraphernalia.

In Central America the custom was handed down by the Mayas to their cultural successors the Toltecs and, later, the Aztecs. Although the power and prestige of the Mayas were fated to fade, their civilization was preserved and enhanced by those who followed them, and the migrations and territorial expansion of the Toltecs and Aztecs spread many earlier Mayan customs—including the use of tobacco—through a large part of present-day Mexico. When Cortez conquered the country in 1519-21, he observed Montezuma and other Aztec chieftains smoking elaborate pipes, although most of the natives used cigars or cigarettes. Just as the conquistadores appear to have plundered most of the Mexican churches and palaces of their principal ornaments and decorations, so also did they carry off the valuable cere-

6

monial pipes, with the result that we know but little of their shape or decoration. The ordinary pipes, recently discovered by archaeologists, were quite simple, usually being merely straight or slightly bent pottery tubes, decorated only with incised lines. The primitive cigar was practically the same as the cigar of today—crushed tobacco leaves rolled in a large leaf of the same plant. Aboriginal cigarettes were also similar to those now in use, except that corn husks, palm leaves and other substitutes, such as short pieces of hollow reed, took the place of the present day paper wrapping.

Throughout the islands of the Caribbean Sea the early explorers found smoking prevalent among the Carib Indians, who also took the finely powdered tobacco leaves as snuff. The Caribs, so we learn from Oviedo's "La Historia General de las Indias," published in 1535, used a hollow Y-shaped piece of cane, the forked ends of which were applied to the nostrils, the other end being placed close to the burning tobacco leaves. This instrument, which was also used for taking snuff, the natives called "tobago" or "tabaco," a name which the Spaniards later applied not only to the cigar but also to the tobacco plant and its cured leaves. The Indians of North, Central, and South America and of the Antilles called the plant and its leaves by a variety of names—cohiba, petum, piecelt, yoli, and uppówac—none of which seems to have become current among the early European visitors to the Western Hemisphere. On the contrary, some form of the Spanish "tabaco" has been incorporated into most of the languages of the world as the ordinary name of the tobacco plant and of its leaves prepared for smoking.

Both snuff-taking and cigar-smoking were practised by the first South American aborigines seen by white men, although in parts of South America, notably in Brazil, pipes were also used. With the exception of the warlike Caribs who lived in some of the Antilles, most of the West Indies and northern and eastern South America were populated by peaceable Indians of the Arawakan linguistic stock who, once having learned to smoke from their neighbors in Central America, had plenty of opportunities to spread the habit among the nearby tribes; being primarily agriculturalists they could easily grow tobacco among their other crops and find leisure to enjoy their cigars or pipes.

Early contacts between the Aztecs of Mexico and the Indians of southwestern North America are attested by the discoveries of Aztec mosaics elaborately worked in turquoise; as turquoise is not found in Mexico itself, the stone must have been brought there from the deposits in the present states of Arizona and New Mexico, a commerce which evidently taught the forebears of our Pueblo and Hopi Indians the pleasures of tobacco. Smoking may also have entered North America by way of the settlements which the Arawakan Indians had made in Florida prior to their expulsion from the West Indies by the Caribs. The extensive travel among the North American Indians— thousand-mile journeys were not uncommon—spread the use of tobacco among practically all of the tribes living in the United States and southern Canada of today. Except in the southwest, where the Mexican form of smoking has always been the most popular, the Indians of North America used pipes rather than cigars; centuries-old trees found growing upon Indian grave mounds in which large quantites of pipes have been found bear silent witness to the antiquity of the tobacco habit among the Red Men of our continent. Large volumes have been written about the pipes of the early North American Indians, who brought the pipe to a point of primitive perfection. Their pipes were of many materials and of many shapes—simple tube pipes, elbow pipes, monitor pipes, effigy pipes and the rest, made of wood, pottery, or one of many different kinds of stone. The various types are of considerable importance, not only because they are valuable examples of the arts and crafts of the aborigines of this continent, but also because the ordinary form of small personal pipe was the prototype of the first pipes smoked in Europe—the famous English clays.

The First Voyage

2

SPAIN MUST HAVE BEEN the first European country to learn about tobacco and smoking, for surely on their return from the Western Hemisphere in 1492 Columbus and the members of his expedition described to their fellow-countrymen the strange Indian custom which they had seen. The earliest written European accounts of smoking are also Spanish, one being contained in Fra Romano Pane's story of his experiences when he accompanied Columbus on his second voyage to the West Indies in 1497, and another being in the "Historia General de las Indias" which the historian Gonzalo Fernández Oviedo y Valdés published in 1535. Neither of these two descriptions of the Indians' use of tobacco was likely to induce many Europeans to adopt the habit. Oviedo wrote that

"Among other evil practises the Indians have one that is especially harmful, the inhaling of a certain kind of smoke . . . in order to produce a state of stupor. . . . The caciques employed a tube, shaped like a Y, inserting the forked extremities in their nostrils, and the tube itself in the lighted weed; in this way they would inhale the smoke until they became unconscious and lay sprawling on the earth like men in a drunken slumber. . . . I cannot imagine what pleasure they derive from this practice, unless it be the drinking which invariably precedes the smoking. . . . It seems to me that here we have a bad and pernicious custom."

Pane's comments were less caustic, but probably quite as incomprehensible to the uninitiated, as he described the Indians' use of the same hollow forked cane in order to snuff tobacco, which, he said, "purges them very much."

The tobacco plant was brought to Spain, where it became highly regarded as a medicinal herb, early in the sixteenth century, but there is considerable difference of opinion as to the identity of its first importer. Credit for having been the first to take the seeds or leaves or slips of the plant to Spain is variously given to Pane and to Oviedo, as well as to Cortez, the conqueror of Mexico, and to Francisco Hernández, a physician sent by King Philip II to study the natural resources of Spain's newly acquired possessions in the New World. Regardless of these conflicting claims, it appears certain that tobacco reached Spain before any other European country. There is no record of tobacco having been elsewhere in Europe prior to 1556, but the Spaniards had gone in for serious tobacco cultivation in the West Indies in 1535, and it is more than probable that within the next two decades some of the Spanish settlers had at least brought samples of their new crop back to their native land.

The only report we have by an actual witness to smoking by the Spaniards in the very early days of the custom is from the pen of Bishop Las Casas; in his "Historia de las Indias" he enlarges somewhat upon the discovery of smoking by de

Jerez and de Torres, already mentioned, and then goes on to say:

> "I knew Spaniards on this island of Española [i.e., San Domingo] who were accustomed to take [tobacco], and being reprimanded for it, by telling them it was a vice, they replied that they were unable to cease using it. I do not know what pleasure or benefit they found in it."

The fact that Las Casas speaks of "reprimanding" the early Spanish smokers for their "vice" seems to bear out the general theory, alluded to in the preface, that the first smokers were probably soldiers, sailors and settlers of the lower grades. Unfortunately, however, this passage does not establish definitely the time when the Spaniards took to tobacco, as Las Casas does not state during what period of his stay in the West Indies, which lasted from 1527 to 1561, he observed the practise. Presumably, however, he refers to some date no later than 1535, for it was apparently in that year that the Spaniards became the first Europeans to cultivate tobacco. Their first plantation was in San Domingo; later others were established in Trinidad, Cuba, Mexico, then in South America and finally in the Philippine Islands. Until the Portuguese began to raise tobacco in their own country in about 1575, to be followed in turn by the Dutch colonists in the East Indies and by the English settlers in Virginia, the Spaniards were the only European tobacco growers and consequently had a virtual monopoly of the continental markets. The Spanish tobaccos from Trinidad and from Varinas, in Colombia, were so highly regarded as to bring as much as eighteen shillings a pound until they were later supplanted in the English markets by the Virginian leaf at about a sixth of that price.

The lack of more accurate information with respect to the beginning of smoking among the Spaniards is less disappointing than it is in the case of the Portuguese, for the Spaniards carried the practice to only a few parts of the world—to western and southern South America and to the Philippines, none of which localities knew tobacco prior to the arrival of the Spanish conquerors. Except for being the first European nation to cultivate the plant, Spain's chief activity in connection with tobacco-smoking was the introduction of the cigar and the cigarette, which the Spaniards had adopted from the natives of the West Indies and Mexico, where the pipe was used relatively rarely. The Spaniards were, however, rather slow in passing the cigar and cigarette on to the pipe-smoking nations; in northern Europe, for example, cigars were practically unknown until almost 1800, and cigarettes did not become at all common until at least fifty years later. These two methods of smoking were therefore rather unimportant factors in the initial spread of tobacco throughout the world.

A Portuguese Mystery

3

IT IS UNFORTUNATE that there is so little information as to when and where tobacco and its use first became known to or was adopted by the Portuguese, for Portugal introduced the custom of smoking to more parts of the world than any other nation. Some years ago an author made a new contribution to the small total of our knowledge about the early history of smoking in Portugal by stating that tobacco had been known there as an article of commerce at least as early as 1523. He based his conclusion on a passage in the will which Diego Columbus, son of Christopher, had executed in 1523, citing a legacy which had been left to one "Antonio, tobacco merchant, a Genoese, who is accustomed to live in Lisbon." This theory completely upset all the existing ideas as to when tobacco was first used in Europe, the general belief previously having been that there had been no commercial demand for tobacco on the continent until about 1550 at the very earliest. Suspicion of the new hypothesis was aroused by the author's quotation of "tobaco mercador", since the correct rendering of "tobacco merchant" would have been "mercador de tabaco." Diligent research, which included an examination of an earlier will written by Diego Columbus in 1506, finally revealed that actually the beneficiary was "Antonioto Baço, mercador", who had subsequently, by poor copying, been transformed into "Antonio, tobaco mercador".

That revolutionary theory having been shattered, students of smoking history found themselves back just where they started, with their knowledge of the early days of tobacco in Portugal limited to the one known fact that it was first seen in that country in 1558, when a Flemish gentleman, Damian de Goes, brought the seeds from Florida and cultivated the lovely plant in his garden at Lisbon. As de Goes was interested only in the beauty and medicinal properties of tobacco, even this item fails to give any clue as to when smoking was first adopted in Portugal.

It is known, however, that by 1555 smoking was a common practice among the Portuguese colonists in Brazil. When, in 1500, Pedro Alvarez Cabral sailed from Portugal on a voyage to India, he was driven so far westward from his intended course that he landed on the coast of Brazil. Although the country had been discovered a year earlier by a Spaniard, Cabral blithely took possession of it in the name of Portugal and reported on its potentialities so enthusiastically that his king sent Amerigo Vespucci to explore the new land. Thereafter, private Portuguese capital financed many colonies in Brazil, which was the only part of the Western Hemisphere with which the Portuguese had any extensive contacts during the sixteenth century. In 1555-6 André Thevet, a Frenchman, visited South America; in the book in which he relates his experiences he described the use of tobacco by the natives of Brazil and added that "all the Europeans" (by which term he could only have meant the Portuguese) "are marvelously eager for this new herb." Although this account indicates that Portuguese settlers in Brazil were smokers by 1555, no one has left any record of the time when they first adopted the habit, nor when and by whom the new custom was brought to Portugal itself.

Jean Nicot

4

THE FIRST NEWS of tobacco to reach France undoubtedly came from Jacques Cartier and his companions on his voyages to North America in search of the fabulous northwest passage to the East Indies. After Cartier had reached Newfoundland and had sailed about the Gulf of the St. Lawrence, he made friends with a tribe of Canadian Indians, two of whom he took back with him on his return to St. Malo in September, 1534. Although in his written report of this first journey Cartier makes no mention of tobacco, it would seem certain that he and his men saw the Indians smoking in Canada and commented on the habit after their return to France.

In May, 1536, Cartier returned to America on a longer expedition, during which he explored the St. Lawrence River as far as the present site of Montreal. In his account of this voyage there occurs the following passage describing the Indians' use of tobacco:

"There groweth also a certain kind of herbe, whereof in Sommer they make great provision for all the yeere, making great account of it, and onely men use of it, and first they cause it to be dried in the Sunne, then weare it about their neckes wrapped in a little beasts skinne made like a little bagge, with a hollow piece of stone or wood like a pipe: then when they please they make pouder of it, and then put it in one of the ends of the said Cornet or pipe, and laying a cole of fire upon it, at the other end sucke so long, that they fill their bodies full of smoke, till that it commeth out of their mouth and nostrils, even as out of the Tonnell of a chimney. They say that this doth keepe them warme and in health: they never goe without some of it about them. We ourselves have tryed the same smoke, and having put it in our mouthes, it seemed almost as hot as Pepper." Cartier's countrymen evidently had no desire to be kept warm and healthy by inhaling such hot fumes, for we find no further mention of tobacco in France for twenty years.

The tobacco plant itself first reached France in 1556, when it was imported from Brazil by André Thevet. Thevet had been in South America from November, 1555 until January, 1556, in company with Villegaignon, who later founded at Rio de Janeiro, under the auspices of Admiral de Coligny, a short-lived colony designed as a haven for the persecuted Hugenots. In his "La cosmographie universelle," published in 1575, Thevet makes the definite claim to have been the first person to bring to France the seeds of this new plant, which the natives of Brazil called "petum"—an onomatopoetic word describing the noise made by the lips during the process of smoking. But Thevet, like Cartier, describes his personal experiences with smoking as having been unpleasant.

A few years after Thevet's return from Brazil there occurred an event which deferred for some time the general adoption of tobacco-smoking in France. Jean Nicot had been sent from Paris in 1559 as Ambassador to the Portuguese court at Lisbon. While at Lisbon he learned about the tobacco plant from Damian de Goes who, as has been mentioned, had been the first to bring tobacco seeds to Portugal. The French Ambassador procured some slips of the plant and grew the herb in his own garden in Portugal; later, it is said, he was successful in using tobacco leaves and their juices to effect cures of ring-worm, ulcer, and cancer—to say nothing of healing a self-inflicted wound of one of his cooks who had cut off "almost all his Thombe . . . with a great Kitchen Knife." Nicot sent seeds and seedlings of the plant to France, and—more important—on his return home in 1561 he persuaded Catherine de' Medici to use as a medicine some of the dried leaves, taken in the form of snuff. His prescription evidently worked satisfactorily, for his remedy found such favor in the eyes of the Queen that for many years the plant was called in France "Herbe de la Reine" and "Herbe Medicée." Eventually, however, these appellations were dropped, and thereafter the botanical designation of the plant was "Nicotiana," named in honor of the French Ambassador.

Catherine de' Medici's use of the herb as snuff put the royal seal of approval on snuffing, which immediately became the correct thing to do throughout the French court. Later most of the courtiers continued the practice despite the fact that Louis XIV disliked tobacco in any form and forbade its use to the members of his personal retinue. Even the king's own physician, for example, remained such a confirmed addict that when—presumably to gain favor in the eyes of his royal patron—he delivered one day a scathing oration denouncing tobacco, he so far forgot himself as to take copious pinches of snuff at the high points of his speech, thereby completely ruining the effect of his tirade. In later years the use of snuff increased and spread further through the upper strata of society; indeed until the nineteenth century snuffing remained the only proper way for the gentlemen of France to take tobacco.

The first Frenchmen known to have been smokers were the Huguenot refugees who in June 1564 established Fort Caroline at the mouth of the St. John's River in Florida. The colony was visited about a year after its founding by Sir John Hawkins, an English sea-captain. In an account of the voyage John Sparke, one of Hawkins' companions, wrote of the use of tobacco by the Indians of Florida and by the French settlers as follows:

" . . . the natives, when they travel have a kind of herbe dryed, which with a cane and an earthen cup in the end, with fire and the dryed herbe together they do suck through the cane the smoke thereof, which smoke satisfieth their hunger, and therewith they live four or five days without meat or drink, and this is all the Frenchmen used for the purpose."

These colonists unfortunately did not live to introduce the tobacco-habit to France, for shortly after Hawkins' visit the entire garrison was slain by the Spaniards. It appears, however, that some of the French Protestants who returned to France from one of the other ill-starred colonies which de Coligny attempted to establish as Huguenot havens—one at Rio de Janeiro founded in 1557, and one at Port Royal in

North Carolina settled five years later— brought the use of tobacco to France. In any event, in 1590 smoking was sufficiently common in France—although not in court circles—so that by that year both French and English students at the University of Leyden in Holland had already made the practice popular among the Dutch.

It Wasn't Raleigh

5

THE HONOR of having been the first person to smoke tobacco in England is claimed for many people. In popular opinion Sir Walter Raleigh leads the field—but he is placed a bad last by all students of the subject. This is about the only point on which the scholars do agree; after that they begin to fight among themselves, each battling for his particular candidate.

The contestant who, in point of time (if we omit the Roman soldiers at Hadrian's Wall) should head the list is Sir John Hawkins, the mariner. His first notable voyage was in 1562-3, when he sailed to the Guinea coast in Africa, robbed the Portuguese slave-traders there, and then sold his captured Negroes in the Spanish possessions in the New World. When he repeated this venture in 1564-5, he ranged along the coast of Florida in search of fresh water on his way home and came upon the colony of French Protestants at Fort Caroline. When Hawkins visited the Huguenot settlement in July, 1565, he and his men became the first Englishmen known to have seen smoking.

The next candidates on the list are Captain Philip Amadas and Captain Arthur Barlowe. In 1584 Sir Walter Raleigh sent these two seamen to America on a search for a place north of the Spanish settlements in Florida which would be suitable for English colonization. They explored the shores of what are now the Carolinas, formally taking possession of the territory in the name of England and naming it Virginia in honor of Queen Elizabeth. Some people believe that after their return Captains Amadas and Barlowe were the first to smoke tobacco in England, while others give this credit to the three Indians whom they had brought back with them.

Further competitors for the honor are Ralph Lane and the settlers who, under his governorship, established the first—but unsuccessful—English colony in America. Largely because of the glowing accounts of Amadas and Barlowe, they had settled at Roanoke Island in North Carolina. After remaining there for about a year, lack of supplies and fear of raids by hostile Indians drove the colonists out, and luckily they were able to take passage to England aboard ships of Sir Francis Drake's fleet on his return, in 1586, from an expedition against the Spanish settlements in the West Indies. Lane and his colonists learned to use tobacco from the Indians and continued to smoke in England on their return. This is vouched for by the "brief and true report of the new found land of Virginia" written by an intimate friend of Sir Walter Raleigh, Thomas Hariot, who had been with the settlers in Virginia; his report contains this account of smoking:

"There is an herbe which is sowed a part by itselfe and is called by the inhabitants uppówac: In the West Indies

23

it hath divers names, according to the severall places &
Countries where it groweth and is used; The Spaniardes
generally call it Tobacco. The leaves thereof being dried
and brought into powder; they use to take the fume or
smoke thereof by sucking it through pipes made of
claie into their stomache and heade; from whence it
purgeth superfluous fleame & other grosse humors,
openeth all the pores and passages of the body: by which
meanes the use thereof, not only preserveth the body
from obstructions; but also if any be, so that they have
not beene of too long continuance, in short time break-
eth them: whereby their bodies are notably preserved in
health, & know not many greevous diseases wherewith-
all wee in England are oftentimes afflicted . . .

"We our selves during the time we were there used to
suck it after their maner, as also since our returne, &
have found manie rare and wonderful experients of the
vertues thereof; of which the relation would require a
volume by itselfe; the use of it by so manie of late, men
& women of great calling as else, and some learned
Phisitions also, is sufficient witnes."

The rest of the stories about the first English smokers are
vague. One account says that Captain William Middleton,
son of the Governor of Denbigh Castle, Wales, Captain
Thomas Price, of Plasyollin, Wales, and a shadowy form
known only as "one Captain Koet" were the first to smoke
in England—but when or where we do not know. After that
all the characters become entirely indefinite, for we are
merely told that "sea captains" or "sailors returned from
America" introduced the habit.

I fail to see why there is so much dispute over the identity of the first person to introduce smoking to England, for it appears certain that this honor should be given to Sir John Hawkins, the first candidate whom we considered. It is true that Sparke wrote nothing about his companions learning to smoke, but neither does he say anything of Hawkins bringing specimens of the tobacco plant to England, although many contemporary authorities agree that he did so. Despite Sparke's omission, a study of the early history of smoking in England leads one inevitably to the conclusion that the men of Hawkins' expedition brought the custom to their native land. The dates tell the story. Hawkins returned from his voyage along the Florida coasts in 1565; the next Englishman to visit the Western Hemisphere was Sir Francis Drake on his voyage against the Spanish strongholds in the West Indies in 1573; Drake was followed in 1584 by Amadas and Barlowe in their exploration of the Carolina shores, where Lane's colony was founded a year later. But earlier than the year of Drake's raids, and before the voyage of Amadas and Barlowe and the expedition under Lane, smoking had taken root in England.

The general adoption of smoking in England is described by contemporary authorities. In the "Stirpium Adversaria Nova," a botanical work published by Doctors Pena and L'Obel in 1570, the authors state that "within these few years" tobacco had become "an inmate of England" and then describe tobacco-smoking thus:

"You see many sailors, and all those who come back from America, carrying little funnels made from a palm leaf or a reed, in the extreme end of which they insert the rolled and powdered leaves of this plant."

Further evidence to the same general effect, although refer-
ring to a few years later, is found in the "Great Chronologie"
which William Harrison finished shortly before his death in
1593. In this year-by-year account of the history of England
we find the following entry under the year 1573:

> "In these daies the taking-in of the smoke of the Indian
> herbe called 'Tabaco', by an instrument formed like a
> litle ladell, whereby it passeth from the mouth into the
> hed and stomach, is gretlie taken-up and used in Eng-
> land. . . . "

Since these reports of eye-witnesses must be taken as irrefut-
able evidence that smoking was prevalent in England at least
as early as 1570 or 1573, it must have been Hawkins, on his
return from America in 1565, who was the first to bring
tobacco to England.

Of all the nations which made their first acquaintance
with tobacco in its native land, England alone wasted no
time in the usual preliminaries of cultivating the plant
merely for its aesthetic or curative values. To be sure, early
English proponents of smoking claimed that the fumes of
tobacco cured such diverse maladies as "Rumes, Catarrahs,
hoarseness, ache in the heade, stomake, lungs, and breast"
and, when taken in the months spelled without an "r",
proved to be a wonderful remedy for "the Megrim, the
toothache, the falling sicknesse, the dropsie, and the gout."
These medicinal attributes of tobacco, however, referred
to its use in pipes, and English tobacco history has but few
parallels to the early continental beliefs in the efficacy of
tobacco-leaf poultices to heal wounds and tobacco juice as a
general panacea. When in 1586 the British first undertook to
raise their own tobacco at Winchcombe, in the Cotswolds,

they did so primarily for just one reason—they wanted the leaves for smoking purposes.

This, I think, was due to the nature of the first English reports on tobacco. Although Hawkins and his men may have regarded tobacco primarily as a substitute for food and drink, as Sparke's account would seem to suggest, they learned of tobacco when they observed fellow-Europeans, as well as Indians, puffing at pipes; early explorers from other countries, on the contrary, first saw smoking only as a strange practice peculiar to the savages of the New World. Amadas and Barlowe themselves experienced the taste of tobacco when they smoked the calumet pipe with the Indian chiefs whom they had encountered. Hariot's report mentions smoking by Lane's colonists not only while they were at Roanoke Island but also after their return to England. These English adventurers, therefore, did not bring home stories about some strange, unpleasant, and rather incomprehensible custom of untutored savages, as was the case with the reports which first reached the other maritime European nations that had had early contacts with the Western Hemisphere. The Englishmen returned with tales of fellow Christians who enjoyed tobacco, and with accounts of their own pleasant experiences with the western habit of smoking.

Although some of the English seamen saw and used the cigar during their voyages in the West Indies, in England pipe-smoking soon became the popular method of taking tobacco. This was only natural, since the principal English contact with the Western Hemisphere was along the southeastern coast of North America, where the Indians were addicted to the use of the various forms of pipes which their craftsmen had developed and where the use of cigars was quite rare. Hence it happens that the English not only adopted the North American manner of smoking but also copied one of the varieties of pipes which they had seen the Indians use.

Many of the Indian pipes were either too elaborate or too large to interest the English as models for their own pipes, especially since the cost of tobacco in England at the time—it sold for what would now amount to over four dollars an ounce—made smoking a very expensive luxury. The British, therefore, ignored the stone and ceremonial pipes and copied the Indians' small personal pottery pipes, some of which the returning colonists undoubtedly brought home with them. Even a cursory comparison of the pictures of the pre-Columbian small Indian pipes of pottery and stone and those of the early English clay pipes will indicate clearly that the Indian personal pipes were the patterns for the first English clays.

The early popularity of pipes in England is attested by Paul Hentzer, a German, who after a visit to England in 1598, wrote that:

> "At these spectacles (he was referring to the Bear Garden at Southwark) and everywhere else, the English are constantly smoking tobacco in this manner: They have pipes on purpose made of clay, into the further end of which they put the herb, so dry that it may be rubbed into powder, and putting fire to it they draw the smoke into their mouths, which they puff out again, through their nostrils, like funnels . . . "

So wedded to their pipes did the English become that when in 1600 the House of Lords tried the Earl of Essex and the Earl of Southampton for high treason, the peers heard the

28

NORTH AMERICAN INDIAN PIPES

*For ordinary, personal use the Indians made small pipes such
as these of pottery or of stone; these specimens range from two
to six inches in length.*

evidence and deliberated upon their verdicts with their pipes going full blast.

Smoking in England, as elsewhere, met stern opposition early in its career. Queen Elizabeth had been content to levy a fairly substantial duty on the importation of tobacco, but her successor, James I, felt that it was high time that the vile habit of smoking was put down. He did not actually forbid his subjects to use tobacco, but in 1603, through his famous "Counterblaste to Tobacco", James let his "deare Countrey-men" know, in very decided terms, that they would incur the royal wrath if they continued to indulge in their "filthie noveltie." After warming up by asserting that smoking did not actually possess the medicinal qualities claimed for it and by deploring the fact that Englishmen had abased themselves "so farre, as to imitate these beastly Indians," he finally let go with both barrels and described smoking as "A custome lothsome to the eye, hatefull to the nose, harmefull to the braine, dangerous to the lungs, and in the black stinking fume thereof, neerest resembling the horrible Stygian smoke of the pit that is bottomeless."

Nor did James stop with inveighing against tobacco. In 1604 he raised the import duty on tobacco from 2d. to 6s. 10d. a pound—an increase of all of 4000%. The true reason for James' antipathy for tobacco is not clear. He could, of course, quote many doctors who thought that smoking was injurious, but medical opinion on that point was sharply divided. At a debate on tobacco arranged when the King visited Oxford in 1605, one brave and worthy physician, puffing furiously on his pipe, swayed all his listeners with his defense of tobacco as a curative. James himself spoke in rebuttal, suggesting, among other things, that all doctors who believed

29

that tobacco had any medicinal virtues might well take themselves and their obnoxious nostrum to join the barbarians of the West Indies who had started the whole depraved business. Perhaps the best clue to the royal attitude towards tobacco is found in the opening sentence of James' edict of 1621 prohibiting the cultivation of the plant in England; this sounds a note of purely personal prejudice when it says: "Whereas we out of the dislike we have of tobacco . . . "

But despite everything that James had done, his subjects had gone right on smoking—so much so that the historian Camden, who obviously shared his sovereign's distaste for tobacco, reported that in 1615:

> " . . . many men, every-where, with an insatiable desire and greediness, sucked in the stinking smoak . . . through an earthen pipe, which presently they blew out again at their nostrils, insomuch that tobacco shops are now as ordinary as tap-houses and taverns."

In the meantime, the British colonists in Virginia had been making small fortunes from tobacco. It is possible that the settlers had grown some of the native North American plant (Nicotiana rustica) which they had seen raised by the Indians, but the initial impetus to the cultivation of tobacco in Virginia came in 1612, when John Rolfe, the husband of Pocahontas, imported to Jamestown seeds of the West Indian variety (Nicotiana tabacum). The latter type proved to be an instant and unqualified success, assuring the financial future of the colony, from which large and lucrative cargoes of the leaf were shipped on every English-bound vessel. A few years later tobacco was even used as currency by the settlers, many of whom, lacking some of the comforts of home, were glad to pay one hundred and twenty pounds of tobacco for the passage of each one of a consignment of a hundred "young women of agreeable persons and respectable character" sent by the London Company as prospective wives for the colonists; as the demand exceeded the supply, the tariff for a second shipload of helpmeets was raised to a hundred and fifty pounds each—making them worth their weight in tobacco, so to speak.

Perhaps it is only fair to revert to Sir Walter Raleigh in order to give him due credit for his activities on behalf of smoking. Although he did not have anything to do with bringing tobacco to England, he was largely responsible for popularizing its use, particularly in fashionable circles. Later he introduced the tobacco plant and its humble relative, the potato, to Ireland. One of his most famous exploits in connection with tobacco was to win a wager from Queen Elizabeth by proving to her that he could weigh smoke. After weighing a fully-charged pipe, he smoked it out, put it on the scales again, and claimed that the difference represented the weight of the smoke. As the Queen ordered the wager paid, she said, "Many alchemists have I heard of who turned gold into smoke, but Raleigh is the first who has turned smoke into gold."

Around the World

6

IT WILL PROBABLY be easier to understand why the Portuguese played such a preëminent part in the propagation of tobacco-smoking throughout the world if we first review briefly Portugal's position in world affairs in the fifteenth and sixteenth centuries.

Those who could bring to the Mediterranean, and thence to the countries of Europe, the cotton, silk, pearls, spices and other luxuries from the East enjoyed a profitable, although dangerous, trade, on which such places as Pisa, Genoa and Venice had grown rich and powerful. But both the overland way through central Asia and the maritime route through the Red and Arabian Seas were so hazardous that the Portuguese, under the guiding genuis of Prince Henry the Navigator, pushed southward in the Atlantic and searched for a way around Africa to the lucrative markets of India and the Near East. Little by little they extended their explorations, consolidating their gains by establishing colonies and trading centers.

The first Portuguese settlement in Africa was effected in 1415 with the capture of Ceuta, just opposite Gibraltar; later Portuguese expeditions took several more seaports along the Atlantic coast of Morocco. By 1480 the Portuguese had explored—and, to a minor extent, colonized—down the western shore of Africa as far as the Gulf of Guinea, from which region many cargoes of gold were brought back to Portugal. Even before Columbus' famous journey to the West Indies, the Portuguese knew all of the Atlantic shores of Africa as far as the mouth of the Congo River, and one Portuguese mariner, Bartolomeu Diaz, had even rounded the Cape of Good Hope and sailed some distance up the eastern coast. In 1497-8 Vasco da Gama followed Diaz' route and continued on to India, where a few years later Cabral landed after the amazing voyage which first had unexpectedly taken him to the South American shores. In the opening years of the sixteenth century the Portuguese founded trading posts on the east coast of Africa and on the western shores of the Indian Peninsula. Then their mariners sailed even further eastward, reaching the Moluccas, in the Malay Archipelago, in 1512, landing in China in 1517, and discovering Japan in 1542.

In the meantime Portuguese colonists had settled along the coast of Brazil, as has been mentioned, and Portugal had entered into friendly diplomatic relations with Persia and Abyssinia. Thus in the middle of the sixteenth century Portugal, at the height of her glory, was not only firmly entrenched on the Brazilian seaboard, but also had a line of scattered possessions along the coasts of East and West Africa, Arabia, India, and the Malay Archipelago and was in a position to dominate the southern trade route between

33

Europe and the East. Portugal maintained her hold on European commerce with Africa, India, China, Japan and the East Indies until it was finally wrested from her about 1600 by the English and Dutch through their East India Companies.

After the Portuguese had established themselves on both the eastern and western shores of the South Atlantic, they carried on an extensive trade between western Africa and Brazil. Vessels engaged in traffic between Portugal and the Ivory and Gold Coasts of Africa found it convenient and profitable to touch at Brazil on both their outward and homeward voyages; not only did they get the benefit of favoring winds by such trans-Atlantic passages, but they also reaped rich rewards by taking slaves from Africa to work on the Portuguese plantations in South America. On their eastward journeys they gradually imported into Africa many of the Brazilian fruits and plants, including, of course, tobacco.

While the Portuguese undoubtedly were the chief propagators of smoking along the West African coastline, it is probable that the natives also learned something of the habit indirectly from the West Indies, either from Spanish traders or from Negro slaves who returned from the Caribbean to their African homes. This assumption is based upon the peculiar fact that in some parts of the Congo region the natives have followed the West Indian custom of naming the pipe itself, rather than the tobacco plant, "tabaco" or "tobago." Generally, however, the West African Negro employs some derivative of "tabaco" for the plant and its leaves, although in another part of the Congo district the unusual use of the word "fumu" (adopted from the Portuguese "fumo", still used in Brazil) for tobacco gives further evidence of a Portuguese-Brazilian importation of the habit and plant into western Africa.

Because one of the first authors to describe this part of Africa fails to make any mention of tobacco in a book on Guinea which he wrote in 1594, it is sometimes inferred that smoking was not known along the shores of the Gulf of Guinea until after the beginning of the seventeenth century, but this position hardly seems tenable. As we shall see later, the Portuguese had undoubtedly introduced smoking into countries further to the East at least by 1600, and surely the chances are that before that time they had started the custom (from which they presumably realized substantial profits) in places closer to their Brazilian source of the plant. Furthermore, contemporary authors tell us of the habitual use of tobacco by the natives of Sierra Leone on the West African coast in 1607 and far up the River Gambia as early as 1620. As it is extremely unlikely that smoking would have become so customary and so wide-spread between 1600 and 1607 or 1620, it seems that the introduction of smoking into these regions by the Portuguese must date from some time in the latter half of the sixteenth century.

The Bushongo natives, living along one of the tributaries of the Congo River, have a pleasant story about the first smoker of their tribe. As the tale goes, one of their tribesmen returned from a journey and proceeded to amaze his fellow townsmen by smoking a pipe. He expatiated on the virtues of the habit by explaining that if a man who had taken offense at someone and therefore harboured murderous ideas of revenge should sit down and smoke a pipe of tobacco, he

35

would reflect and decide that thrashing would be a more proper vengeance than killing; after further consideration over a second pipe he would determine on scolding instead of physical punishment, and at the end of the third pipe he would find it in his heart to forgive his fellow and forget the whole incident.

꧁ ꧂

To Diaz, da Gama, Cabral, and the other Portuguese mariners who rounded the Cape of Good Hope, the southern tip of Africa seemed to have scant commercial possibilities, so their countrymen made no settlements between the present land of Angola on the Atlantic seaboard and Portuguese East Africa on the east coast. But along the African shores of the Indian Ocean they established trading centers as early as 1501, and later in the century they penetrated inland along the Zambezi River. As their trade with this part of Africa was not very large—they preferred the gold of the west African coast, or the spices and silks of India and the Far East—the Portuguese introduction of smoking to the Negroes of eastern Africa occurred considerably later than was the case on the opposite side of the continent, and it took a longer time for the habit, once introduced, to spread itself throughout the territory.

꧁ ꧂

While the Portuguese were thus engaged in monopolizing trade—and, as a side-line, introducing the tobacco habit —along the seacoasts of Africa, they had also become important factors in Abyssinia. For centuries European rulers had been hoping to find the kingdom of the mythical eastern Christian monarch known as Prester John; when finally it was rumoured that his empire was not in the Far

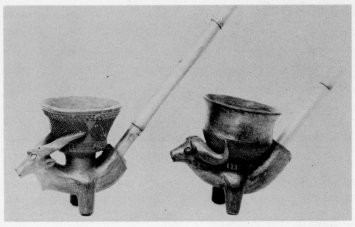

PIPES FROM SOUTHEASTERN AFRICA

Most of the African tribes evolved their own peculiar pipe forms; those shown here are designed to rest upon the ground while being smoked through three-foot bamboo stems.

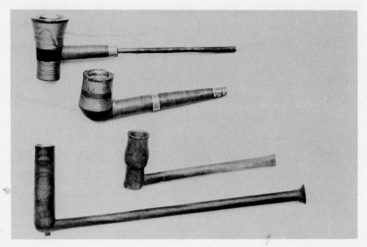

PIPES FROM SOUTH AFRICA

The European influence on South African pipes is exemplified by these specimens.

East, but in Abyssinia, a Portuguese expedition went via the Mediterranean and thence across Africa in search of the fabulous potentate, reaching Abyssinia in 1490. Although the Portuguese must soon have realized that they had not found the object of their quest, they remained in the country for almost a century and a half, teaching Christianity to the Ethiopians and helping them to repel their Mohammedan invaders. When political intrigue finally forced them to leave Abyssinia in 1633, the Portuguese left behind them the tobacco plant and the practice of smoking.

Abyssinia appears to have the distinction of having been under the most recent prohibition of smoking. In many other countries tobacco was interdicted shortly after its introduction, but it was not until the end of the last century that a decree forbidding smoking was issued in Abyssinia. This edict was not based on medical theories nor on pseudo-religious grounds nor on any of the other objections to tobacco usually put forward in support of such taboos. The reason was much simpler. According to the story, the Emperor of Abyssinia one day decided to try a pipe of tobacco for the first time—and promptly suffered the same acutely unpleasant experience that has been the lot of so many juveniles when they sneaked their first smokes from cigarettes or cigars pilfered from their elders' humidors. The Emperor immediately decided that it would be *lèse-majesté* for his subjects to enjoy a habit which had given their sovereign such pain and forthwith prohibited the use of tobacco in his kingdom, for which he was made an honorary member of the Anti-Tobacco Society of France. It is hardly necessary to add that the edict soon became a dead letter.

When the Portuguese became interested in the commercial possibilities of the east coast of Africa shortly after 1500, they apparently found it easier to capture existing Arabian trading stations along those shores than to establish settlements of their own. Accordingly, they seized several Arab posts in that vicinity and even took possession later of a considerable portion of Arabia itself along the Arabian Sea and the Gulf of Oman. These aggressive measures served the dual purpose of hampering the trade of the Arabs, who were one of Portugal's principal competitors in the trade between the Orient and Europe, and of giving the Portuguese themselves convenient bases from which to carry on their own commerce with the East.

As the use of tobacco was spread by both martial and peaceful relations between nations, it is not strange that their hostile contacts with the Portuguese taught the Arabs how to smoke. That Portugal was the source of the smoking habit among the Arabians is clearly shown by the fairly common use by the Arabs of the word "Bortugal" for tobacco. Although there seem to be no native records of the date when smoking was introduced into Arabia, there is some reliable outside evidence on that point. The Hindu courtier Asad Beg, whose story of bringing the first pipes to northern India is mentioned later, wrote that another member of his Emperor's retinue knew that tobacco was being cultivated at the Arabian cities of Mecca and Medina in 1605. It therefore is safe to assume that the Portuguese had started the practice of smoking among the Arabians by 1600 at the very latest.

The Portuguese had little or nothing to do with the introduction of tobacco into most of northern Africa and into southern Africa. It seems best, however, to discuss at this point the beginnings of the use of tobacco in those regions, in order to keep some geographical continuity when it is not feasible to trace the course of smoking around the globe by following in the footsteps of the different nations—Portugal, England, and Spain—who were its principal apostles.

The northern part of Africa, from the Red Sea to the Atlantic, held an amazing conglomeration of peoples in the latter half of the sixteenth century. Several hundred years earlier a fanatical Mohammedan host had swept westward from Arabia and had conquered all the Mediterranean coast between their home and the Atlantic. In the first half of the sixteenth century the Turks in their turn overran northern Africa, overcoming Egypt, Tripoli, Tunisia, and most of Algeria except for a few seaports which had been captured by the Spaniards. The Spaniards also dominated one or two Mediterranean coast towns in Morocco, while the Portuguese held almost all of the Moroccan ports on the Atlantic. Despite the activities of the pirates of the Barbary Coast, Italy had an extensive commerce with Tunisia and Tripoli, and the Moors, ever appreciative of the advantages of foreign trade, had entered into diplomatic relations with the European powers, one of whom—France—had sent an ambassador to Morocco as early as 1570.

With such a mixture of races in a territory so wild, it is no wonder that it is difficult to trace the course of smoking through the region. Fortunately, however, an Arabian writer of the times states definitely that in 1601 to 1603 smoking began to be practiced by the Egpytians, who doubtless had learned the habit from their Turkish or Arabian neighbors further to the east. Further westward along the southern shores of the Mediterranean the smoking customs are still so similar to those of Egypt that we must infer that the habit came into such countries as Tripoli and Tunisia from the East rather than from the North; after all, since the Italians generally did not take up smoking until after 1610, it is doubtful whether they would have transplanted the practice to the Barbary Coast before it had reached there from Egypt.

Both the eastern and the European nations were influential in Algeria and the countries further westward, but it seems extremely likely that the Portuguese introduced the tobacco habit along the Atlantic shores of Morocco. On the other hand, central Morocco, we are told, received its first tobacco from Timbuktu, to which the plant could have penetrated only northward from the Negroes of the west African coast and the Gulf of Guinea, whither it had first been brought by the Portuguese. Tobacco was taken throughout the Sahara and the Sudan by the caravans which, thanks to the camels imported from Arabia, set out from the northern cities and traversed the deserts. South of these regions, save along the coasts, the traders from the north could not go, being stopped by the dense forest belt which crosses the Dark Continent somewhat north of the Equator—but in the wilds of Africa the Negroes themselves rapidly spread the custom of smoking from tribe to tribe.

For over a century after its discovery, South Africa was ignored, as far as colonization went, by the Portuguese and the other Europeans who followed them around the Cape of Good Hope to the rich commercial fields in the East. Although their vessels frequently watered at Table Bay, neither the explorers nor the traders felt that this relatively poor section of the continent was worth developing until the Netherlands East India Company made the first formal attempt at annexation and settlement in 1652. At their direction, a small force of colonists under Jan van Riebeck founded Cape Town, the first permanent European foothold in that part of the continent.

The Kaffirs and Hottentots became acquainted with tobacco-smoking only through the medium of the Hollanders. This conclusion is supported by the fact that a common form of native pipe closely resembles the Dutch type, as well as by accounts of persons who visited the country not long after 1652. Their reports, which definitely attribute to the Dutch the introduction of smoking into that region, are particularly interesting as proof of how rapidly the natives—women and children as well as men—became passionately addicted to the habit. Early narratives relate that the Hottentot gladly sold his sheep or his bullock for a twisted rope of tobacco that was as long as the animal itself, and that in some cases the Dutch, as they advanced further northward, were able to buy the natives' land for the same currency—and precious little of it, at that.

For many years after the Portuguese had first established trading stations on the western shores of India in 1501, they continued to be the most influential Europeans in that region. Their merchants carried on an active trade with the Hindus, whom Portuguese missionaries labored to convert to Christianity, and at some time before the end of the sixteenth century the Portuguese brought the tobacco habit to India.

The earliest native story of smoking in India describes an incident which took place in 1605 at Delhi. The tale was written by Asad Beg, an officer of the court of Emperor Akbar. According to Asad Beg, he had bought some pipes and tobacco at Bijapur, in southern India, and on his return to Delhi offered to his emperor a smoke from a pipe which he describes as having a jeweled stem over four feet long, finished with a mouthpiece of carnelian. We do not know if Akbar adopted the habit after his first experience with it, but at least he did not frown upon the new custom, for Asad Beg says that he made presents of pipes and tobacco to other nobles of the court and thus started the new fashion, which gained adherents daily.

Since Asad Beg had been able to buy "a large supply of tobacco and pipes" in the bazars at Bijapur, smoking obviously was quite common in the southern part of India in 1605. The habit therefore must have been first brought to India several years earlier—probably before the end of the sixteenth century—by the Portuguese merchants and missionaries who had settled at Goa, Cochin and Calicut on the western seaboard.

The Emperor Akbar was succeeded in 1605 by his son Jehangir, who ruled until 1627. Jehangir, so we are told in his own writings, felt obliged to copy the example set by his brother Shah Abbas of Persia, and forbid the use of the "pernicious plant introduced by the Europeans." The form of punishment which he adopted was a relatively mild one for an eastern potentate of those days; he merely decreed that anyone found smoking should have his lips slit so that he could no longer indulge in the habit.

It would be pleasant if careful research supported the proponents of the theory that the Portuguese introduced tobacco into Japan in 1542, for that would mean that Europeans had taken the practice of smoking half way around the world in exactly fifty years after it had first become known to them. Besides, the story on which this hypothesis is based is a romantic one, for it concerns a series of adventures through which some Portuguese travelers accidentally became the first Europeans to set foot in Japan. Before their visit the country had been known to Europeans only from the hearsay descriptions of "Zipangu, rich in gold" which Marco Polo had brought back after his journeys to China at the end of the thirteenth century.

In 1542 Fernão Mendes Pinto, an adventurer who in the course of an eventful life was captured and sold into slavery no less than seventeen times, and seven other Portuguese found themselves stranded at a Chinese port. As the only possible means of returning to the Moluccas, in the East Indies, they finally took passage on two Chinese pirate junks. After a sea fight with the ships of a rival pirate force, a storm wrecked one of the junks and drove the other, on which were Pinto and two of his compatriots, to a strange seacoast, where the corsairs and their Portuguese companions landed. Their refuge proved to be Japan. The Japanese who met them received the voyagers most hospitably and questioned the Portuguese at great length about the things which they had seen on their travels throughout the world. The Orientals learned of at least one European invention from the strangers to their shores, for they were so interested in the potentialities of the arquebus with which the Portuguese were armed that they copied the new weapon and had manufactured over six hundred of them before Pinto and his companions left the island half a year later. There is, however, absolutely no evidence that these particular Portuguese taught the Japanese how to use tobacco as well as firearms, for Pinto's own account of his travels, in which he relates his visit to Japan in considerable detail, makes no mention of any such incident. Indeed, it is not certain that any Portuguese had begun to smoke as early as 1542, and it is not until after many years of commerce between the Japanese and the Portuguese that the written records of Japan mention either tobacco or smoking.

The earliest reference to tobacco in any Japanese document occurs in a town register of land assessment, in which some entries for the years 1578-1579 refer to one of the landowners as being a "tobacco merchant."

The next Japanese mention of tobacco is for the year 1607, under which date the journal kept by a Doctor Saka contains the following item:

"Of late a thing called tobacco has been in fashion. It is said to have come from Nañbañ. Broad leaves are cut up and lighted and the smoke is swallowed."

The doctor's diary seems to be the only document available as a contemporary description of the beginning of smoking in Japan. While it is probably not entirely accurate as to the date when the Nipponese started to smoke, it is of considerable interest in its testimony as to the Portuguese origin of the habit. The term "Nañbañ," which literally means "southern barbarians," was applied by the Japanese to most Occidental foreigners, including the Portuguese, Spanish and other Europeans; in this instance, however, the Portuguese are certainly the people indicated, since for over half

44

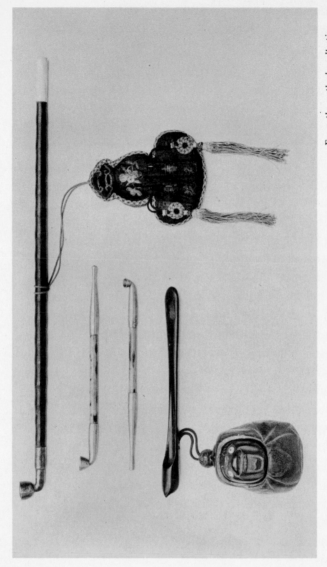

ASIATIC PIPES

A Chinese pipe with a silken tobacco pouch; a Korean pipe; a Japanese pipe with a wooden pipe-holder and tobacco box.

a century after they had discovered Japan the Portuguese were the only Europeans who enjoyed any extensive intercourse with the Japanese.

Although the diary just quoted contains valuable evidence as to the Portuguese source of smoking in Japan, the doctor's testimony as to the time when the Japanese began to smoke is probably faulty. There is a strong reason to believe, even though the information does not come from contemporary sources, that the seeds of tobacco were brought to Japan by the Portuguese sometime between 1573 and 1592, that smoking was fairly common on the island as early as 1595, and that the plant was cultivated at Ebusuki by 1596 and at Nagasaki in 1605. These data give further weight to the belief that in 1578 smoking may have been fairly general in Japan and that tobacco may have been a regular article of commerce by that time, as is indicated by the "tobacco merchant" entry in the land records mentioned above.

Tobacco-smoking soon fell into disrepute in Japan and was banned. This came about largely because of the unpleasant activities of two organizations known as the Bramble Club and the Leather Breeches Club, both of which were originally formed as smoking societies; their members affected pipes which were so long and heavy that they were either worn in the sash like swords or carried by retainers. The chief delight of these gay young blades was to provoke the ordinary citizens of the town into quarrels which developed into such unpleasant street brawls that finally the authorities had to put an end to their belligerent form of amusement by the execution of a dozen of the ringleaders. The popular resentment against the roisterers had extended even to their habit of smoking, and therefore the Dud

45

Shogun issued—in 1612—the first Japanese edict banning the cultivation and use of tobacco. Similar royal prohibitions of smoking appeared periodically in later years, apparently based on more logical criticisms of the habit, such as the danger of fire from pipe ashes, the theory that smoking was prejudicial to the general health, and the fear that the cultivation of tobacco in Japan would seriously interfere with the production of the more vital crops of rice and corn. The frequency with which these laws were issued testifies to the failure of tobacco taboos in Nippon; the people ran the risk of suffering the rather mild penalities, such as the confiscation of property, and smoking continued to grow in popularity and to spread further throughout Japan in spite of all the pronouncements against it.

In 1592 the Japanese successfully invaded the Korean peninsula. Their victory was assured at the outset of the campaign, for the Japanese were able to equip some of their soldiers with the arquebuses which they had copied from the firearms carried by Pinto and the other first Portuguese visitors to their island. When the Japanese suddenly and inexplicably withdrew from Korea, they left behind them one of the pleasanter aspects of European civilization—smoking.

The Koreans adopted the Japanese type of pipe, and even today there is a close similarity between the Korean and Japanese instruments. Another witness as to the origin of smoking among the Koreans is their word for tobacco, which is "Nambankoy," based on the Japanese word "Nañbañ," which has just been mentioned.

Three different peoples, of whom the Portuguese were one, introduced tobacco into China.

After the Portuguese had first landed in China in 1517, and particularly after they had founded a small colony near Canton in 1567, they developed a substantial trade with the Chinese, from which the later European arrivals in China were largely excluded. Certainly the Portuguese must have acquainted the Chinese, as they did so many other people, with the use of tobacco, but, perhaps because the Portuguese confined their commerce with China to only one or two southern seaports, Lady Nicotine's debut in China under their auspices seems to have been only a small, local affair.

In reaching China, tobacco had girdled the globe, for it came there not only from the East, through the medium of the Portuguese, but also from the West, via the Philippine Islands, to which the Spaniards had brought the seeds across the Pacific from Mexico. The importation of tobacco into China from the Philippines about the year 1600 is attested by a contemporary poet and essayist who wrote:

"There is a plant called tan-pa-ku produced in Luzon . . . You take fire and light one end and put the other end in your mouth. The smoke goes down your throat through the pipe. It can make one tipsy, but it can [likewise] keep one clear of malaria. People have brought it to [Fu-kien] and planted it, and now there is more than in Luzon, and it is exported and sold to that country. It is commonly called gold-silk-smoke."

Tobacco went to China from the Philippines not only directly, from Luzon to Fu-kien, but also indirectly, by way of the island of Formosa. The close similarity between present-day Philippine and Formosan pipes, and the existence in both places of the unusual custom by which pipes often are used merely as cigar-holders, clearly indicate the Philippine origin of smoking in Formosa. It is peculiar, by the way, that the small island of Botol-Tobago-Shima, lying between Formosa and the Philippines, is the home of one of the few known races of the world who will have absolutely nothing to do with tobacco, although presumably these islanders have known of the plant and its use for several centuries.

The people of Manchuria had also learned of the pleasure of tobacco about 1600 from the Koreans and had quickly passed it on to their Chinese neighbors to the south and west. The Manchurians, indeed, appear to have influenced Chinese smoking customs far more than either the Portuguese or the Filipinos, for Chinese pipes closely resemble those used in Japan and Korea, whence the tobacco habit had made its way to Manchuria. The usual form of pipe throughout China, Japan and Korea consists of a tiny metal bowl (made small apparently because of the early habit of mixing a little opium with the tobacco) and a slender metal mouthpiece, joined to the bowl by a bamboo stem. Aside from certain native differences in the decorations on the better pipes, practically the only distinction between the Japanese and the Korean pipes on the one hand, and the Chinese pipes on the other, is in the size, which is considerably larger in China than in the two other countries. Even this is a rather minor distinction, for some of the early Japanese pipes were, as has been stated, almost as long as swords and were occasionally made so stoutly as to form a rather formidable weapon when wielded by a strong right arm.

48

As was the case in Japan, prohibitions of smoking were issued in China periodically—in 1637, 1638, 1640, and 1643—and ineffectually; not even decapitating tobacco sellers and exposing their heads on pikes could put a stop to the clandestine traffic in tobacco. Once the Chinese along the seaboard became tobacco addicts, they promptly spread the habit throughout other parts of Asia. Chinese merchants traveled extensively through eastern Siberia, Mongolia, Tibet and Turkestan and left in their wake not only the custom of smoking, but also Chinese tobacco, Chinese smoking utensils, and even words for tobacco and pipes derived from the Chinese language.

The Portuguese were the first Europeans to reach the islands of the Malay Archipelago, discovering Java, Sumatra, New Guinea, Celebes and the Moluccas early in the sixteenth century. For some years thereafter they practically monopolized the trade with most of these islands. Their first would-be rivals were the Spanish, who tried to uphold their claim that some of the islands lay within their sphere of exploration and exploitation as laid down by the Treaty of Tordesillas. This rather extraordinary pact, which reaffirmed, with modifications, two papal bulls issued by Pope Alexander VI in 1493, was based on a theoretical bisection of the globe, quite like cutting an apple in two. All future discoveries lying in the western half were to belong, when and if found, to Spain, while Portugal was given a similar title to all lands which might be discovered in the eastern half; the other European nations, as well as the natives of the new countries, were calmly ignored. There was, from the standpoint of the Spaniards and Portuguese, only one flaw in this arrangement—the geographers of the day were unable to say exactly where the lines of demarcation lay. The argument over the title to some of the islands of Malaysia, which fell within a controversial area, was settled in 1529 in favor of the Portuguese, who thereafter held undisputed sway until the star of their empire suddenly declined about the close of the sixteenth century. Then the Dutch and the English became active factors in Malaysia, first as independent adventurers and merchants, and later as members of the powerful Dutch and British East India companies; of these traders, the Hollanders were by far the more important in making their influence felt throughout the archipelago.

Since the Portuguese had introduced the tobacco habit into so many of the eastern countries with which they had established trade relations, it is only natural to infer that they taught the natives of Malaysia to smoke. However, many authorities are inclined to the opinion (although on somewhat scanty evidence) that it was the Dutch, rather than the Portuguese, who brought smoking to the Malay Archipelago. Their theory is supported by the fact that the Portuguese contented themselves merely with trading among these islands and did not actually annex any territory nor found their own colonies, as they did in such other places as Africa, India, and China. A further argument in favor of the Dutch introduction of tobacco is that the few known dates of the inception of the habit in these countries—Java in 1601, Celebes in 1613, and the Moluccas about 1615—are after the Portuguese power had waned and had been supplanted by Dutch supremacy in the East. One writer on smoking in Java says that tobacco was "probably introduced there by the Portuguese and possibly re-introduced later by

NEW GUINEA SMOKING TUBES

*At the top of each tube may be seen the small hole in which
the cigarette is inserted.*

the Hollanders"—a phrase which, I think, could properly be applied to almost all of the Malay Archipelago, thereby dividing between the Portuguese and the Dutch the credit for having brought the practice of smoking to these islands.

There are two important exceptions to this statement—the Philippine Islands and New Guinea. Travelers who visited New Guinea in 1615 found the inhabitants already accustomed to the use of tobacco. As up to that time there had been little or no European contact with the island, the natives must have learned of the pleasures of tobacco from some of their Pacific neighbors—presumably from the Philippines, where the Spaniards had introduced smoking about 1575. Indeed, the indirect Spanish influence on the tobacco customs of New Guinea is still evident in the current popularity of the cigarette among the natives. Along the northern coast, where pipes are not used at all, cigarettes are made by wrapping loose tobacco in banana leaves, hibiscus leaves, or even—if it is available—in newspaper. Of the typical native pipes, one form is merely a copy of a European type, and most of the others are really cigarette holders. One interesting variety, for example, is a two or three foot section of bamboo, closed at one end and open at the other, with a small hole into which the cigarette is inserted; one man draws at the open end of the pipe until it is full of smoke, when he removes the cigarette, closes the open end of the tube with his hand, and passes the pipe to the others in the company, who inhale the smoke from the small hole which had held the cigarette.

Portugal did more than any other nation to spread the use of tobacco over the face of the world. In a little more than the period of time covered by the last quarter of the sixteenth century, the Portuguese had introduced smoking to the east and west African coasts, Abyssinia, Arabia, India, Japan, China, and the Malay Archipelago—in short, to all the countries where Portuguese colonists and merchants had established themselves along their trade routes that led to the opposite side of the earth. Thanks to the Portuguese and to the Spaniards, when tobacco reached China the custom of smoking had actually encircled the globe in about a century after the European nations had first discovered the "divine herb."

Commerce and War

7

THE ENGLISH appear to have taken to smoking, once they had made the acquaintance of tobacco, more rapidly and more enthusiastically than almost any other European people; having become ardent smokers, they then were second only to the Portuguese in teaching their new habit to other nations.

Their first pupils were the Dutch—and very apt pupils they were, judging by the subsequent consumption of tobacco in the Netherlands. The use of tobacco was introduced into Holland shortly before 1590, as William van der Meer, a physician of Delft, wrote in 1621 that he had first seen smoking in 1590, when he found that the English and French students at the University of Leyden had already made pipe-smoking a common practice. The Dutch soon became so addicted to the habit that by 1610 tobacco was one of the country's principal imports, by 1615 the Dutch had laid out, at Amersfoort, the first tobacco plantation in Europe, and by 1620 they were the largest European consumers of and dealers in tobacco.

Many years afterwards it was a Hollander, Mynheer van Klaes, who won the title—unofficial—of the "King of Tobacco", largely by consuming the rather staggering total of an estimated four tons of tobacco in the course of his long and successful career. In his will he asked that all the smokers of the country be invited to attend his funeral and be requested to smoke throughout the ceremony. When the coffin, lined with the fragrant wood of cigar-boxes, was lowered into the grave, the mourners scattered the ashes of their pipes on the lid and filed out of the cemetery, to receive each one a present of ten pounds of tobacco and two new pipes engraved with the benefactor's name and crest. It would be interesting to know whether van Klaes' will and fortune stood the test of time well enough so that all the poor of the neighborhood who attended his funeral actually did receive, until their deaths, their stipulated legacies of annual gifts of large packages of tobacco.

Chronologically, the second country to which the English introduced tobacco was Turkey. The first contemporary story of smoking there was written by John Dallam, an English organ builder who visited Constantinople in 1599—perhaps in order to try to supply an Anglo-Saxon form of soft music for the harems. Dallam's journal says that when his ship was nearing Constantinople it was stopped by a Turkish naval vessel, the captain of which boarded the merchantman and requested the Englishmen to make him presents of tobacco and tobacco-pipes.

That the English were the principal sellers of tobacco to the Turks is also indicated in the diary of another English traveler, George Sandys, who visited Constantinople in 1611.

In his "Relation of a Journey begun A. D. 1610" Sandys wrote that the Turks

" . . . delight in Tobacco: which they take thorow reeds that have ioyned unto them great heads of wood to containe it—I doubt not but lately taught them, as brought them by the English: and were it not sometimes lookt into (for Morat Bassa not long since commanded a pipe to be thrust thorow the nost of a Turke, and so to be led in derision thorow the City), no question but it would prove a principall commodity. Neverthelesse they will take it in corners; and are so ignorant therein, that that which in England is not saleable, doth passe here amongst them for most excellent."

From these two reports it is evident that the Turks had learned of smoking before 1599, that the English were important factors in supplying them with tobacco, and that by 1611 the habit had become sufficiently widespread to provoke a royal edict against it. Tobacco continued to grow in popularity among the Turks, however, and smoking became a common practice, particularly in the coffee-houses, until suddenly Murad IV started a ruthless campaign against the custom.

Murad IV was a rather contradictory character who wrote light verses and death warrants with equal ease and with about equal frequency. It is said that once this gigantic Ottoman Sultan caused a thousand Persian captives to be executed simultaneously before his tent, and during his reign (from 1623 to 1640) over a hundred thousand of his subjects are supposed to have been killed for infringing his rules, or in some other fashion attracting the unfavorable notice of their sovereign. Partly because he himself disliked smoking, partly in order to discourage gatherings in which malcontents discussed the sad state of affairs under his rule, and partially on the pretext that careless smokers had caused the great Constantinople conflagration in 1633, he forbade his subjects to smoke. His crusade was given a religious backing when it was announced that several centuries earlier Mohammed had prophesied that in later days some of his followers would stray from the paths of righteousness so far as to smoke an herb which would be known as tobacco—an astounding piece of clairvoyance, if only it could be believed. The punishment for violating the royal prohibition was death, usually in a most unpleasant form—a penalty which was inflicted upon as many as eighteen culprits in a single day. In those days many monarchs seemed to think it unnecessary to practice what they preached, so perhaps it would be charitable to say that Murad IV was only exercising one of his royal prerogatives when one learns that although he had prohibited the use of wine, as well as of tobacco, coffee, and opium, his own death was caused by gout brought on by excessive drinking.

From Turkey the practice of smoking went to Persia, which was one of the countries to learn the habit as a result of war. In the sixteenth and seventeenth centuries Turkey and Persia were continually waging campaigns against each other. Sultan Murad IV led his armies—incidentally, he was the first Ottoman ruler to take that advanced position with his troops in actual battle—on many expeditions into Persia, and it appears to have been from such hostile contacts with their neighbors that the Persians became acquainted with tobacco. The date when they gained this new knowledge is uncertain, but presumably it was after 1600, for the literature of Persia contains no mention of tobacco prior to that date. By 1626, however, an English traveler reported that Persians of both sexes and of all classes smoked everywhere, even in the mosques, and by 1636, the Persians were growing their own tobacco, which later became, as the famous Shiraz tobacco, one of the finest varieties of the world.

The accounts of eye witnesses of the early popularity of smoking in Persia serve to emphasize how fruitless were most attempts to outlaw smoking. Because they believed that the use of tobacco made men sterile and consequently were fearful that the birth rate of their nation would decrease alarmingly if their subjects continued to smoke, both Shah Abbas the Great, in whose reign the habit apparently first came to Persia, and his successor, Shah Sufi, did everything they could to stop the use of tobacco, the latter prescribing the peculiarly unpleasant punishment of pouring molten lead down the throats of persons caught smoking. Even such extreme penalties failed to prevent the tobacco habit from spreading throughout the length and breadth of Persia at the very time when the royal prohibitions were still being strictly enforced.

A particularly interesting method of smoking is the eastern use of apparatus by which the smoke is drawn through water before being inhaled. This practice is so generally associated with the Turks that the mention of a water-pipe immediately conjures up for the average person mental images of Turkish sultans seated cross-legged in their harems, completely surrounded by the weaving forms of dancing girls and the octopus-like coils of the tubes of their bubbling hookahs. It is true that the Turkish hookah is not only one of the most elaborate and ornamental forms of water-pipes but also one of the best known, having at one time been quite popular in some eastern European countries, notably Germany and Russia. But the Turk is only one of many African and Asiatic peoples who smoke in this manner today. The Persian uses a water pipe made of copper or brass known as a "kalian"; the Hindu puffs at a coco-nut "nargileh" or at a "hubble-bubble" made of clay; the African Negro fashions a water-pipe from an eland's horn, and the Chinese have evolved their own unique and graceful form of small metal water-pipe.

There is a theory that many years before tobacco had been introduced to the Dark Continent the African Negro had invented the water-pipe as a means for smoking hemp. However, it is more than likely that hemp, which is indigenous to India, did not reach Africa until after the Europeans had acquainted the Negroes with tobacco; moreover, regardless of the date of the first use of hemp by the Africans or by anyone else, it is very doubtful whether any users of that narcotic actually smoked hemp before they had learned about smoking tobacco, for they probably took hemp either in liquid form or in pills.

A more logical theory about the origin of the water-pipes—and one which has yet to be disproved—was the first one advanced. This is contained in one of the earliest books devoted entirely to tobacco, published in 1622 by the celebrated physician Johann Leander and entitled "Tobacologia . . . a medico-surgico-pharmaceutical description of tobacco . . ." Its author describes and pictures a Persian kalian and definitely attributes the invention of the water-pipe to the Persians.

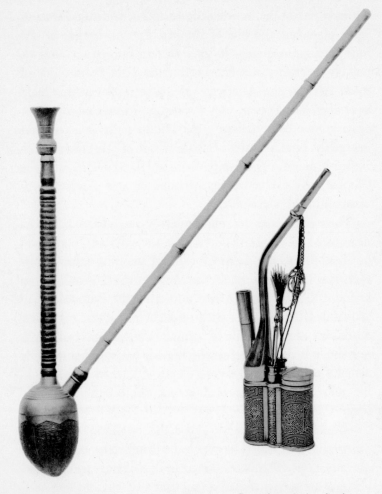

WATER PIPES

*The nargileh, with a coconut base, is about twenty inches tall.
The metal water pipe, from China, has the advantage of being
easily portable.*

While the English are credited with having brought the use of tobacco to Russia, presumably along the shores of the Baltic, the Turks also played an important part in teaching the custom to the Muscovites, for the Turkish word for tobacco was incorporated into the Russian language. Furthermore, the use of the water-pipe was at one time much more extensive in Russia than it was in any of the other European countries to which the Turks—without any lasting effect—had introduced that particular method of smoking.

The Russians probably began to use tobacco sometime between 1610 and 1620, for it was in 1634 that Czar Michael Feodorovitch Tourieff issued the first Russian edict against smoking. The Russian prohibition, like the Turkish, had spiritual support, thanks to the conveniently manufactured tradition that it was with the fumes of tobacco, rather than with wine, that the devil had made Noah drunk. The temporal arm inflicted severe penalties on culprits; for the first offense the smoker suffered the knout, for the second he lost his nose, and for the third—and obviously the last—he lost his head.

Tobacco was first taken to Italy as a medicinal plant by the Papal Nuncio Prospero Santa Croce, who on his return from the Portuguese court at Lisbon in 1561 brought back some of the seeds of the new herb. At about the same time another Papal Nuncio, Nicolo Tornabuoni, who was in Paris from 1560 to 1565 as Ambassador from Tuscany, reported to the Grand Duke of Tuscany on the curative properties of the plant just introduced into Paris by Nicot and also sent some of the seeds to Florence. For some years the

59

tobacco plant was known in Italy either as "herba Santa Croce" or "erbe Tornabuona", in honor of the men who had first brought it to the country.

Although it seems as though many Italian seamen, like those of the other European maritime nations of the day, must have known of and perhaps practiced smoking during the latter half of the sixteenth century, the habit did not gain any real foothold in Italy until after 1610. Possibly this is due to the extremely unfavorable report on the practice made by Giralamo Benzoni of Milan, who traveled in the Western Hemisphere from 1541 to 1556, and who wrote what appears to be the first Italian account of smoking. In his "History of the New World" Benzoni gives the following description of the use of tobacco by the natives of the Western Hemisphere and by the slaves brought there by the Spaniards:

"When these leaves are in season, they pick them, tie them up in bundles, and suspend them near their fire-place till they are very dry; and when they wish to use them, they take a leaf of their grain (maize), and putting one of the others into it, they roll them round tight together; then they set fire to one end, and putting the other end into the mouth, they draw their breath up through it, wherefore the smoke goes into the mouth, the throat, the head, and they retain it as long as they can, for they find a pleasure in it; and so much do they fill themselves with this cruel smoke, that they lose their reason. And there are some who take so much of it, that they fall down as if they were dead, and remain the greater part of the day or night stupefied. Some men are found who are content with imbibing only enough of this smoke to make them giddy, and no more.

See what a wicked and pestiferous poison from the devil this must be. It has happened to me several times that, going through the provinces of Guatemala and Nicaragua, I have entered the house of an Indian who had taken this herb, which in the Mexican language is called 'tabacco,' and immediately perceiving the sharp fetid smell of this truly diabolical and stinking smoke, I was obliged to go away in haste, and seek some other place." It is no wonder that, with such unfavorable publicity, smoking did not become popular in Italy for many years.

The use of tobacco did not become general in Italy until Cardinal Crescenzio returned to Italy in 1610 from his travels, during which he had learned to smoke while in England. Under the auspices of such an exalted personage, both tobacco-smoking and the use of snuff were quickly adopted by all classes, so much so that the custom became common throughout Italy in a very few years. Unfortunately both the clergy and the laity soon used tobacco so incessantly that they began to smoke and take snuff even in the churches, which led Pope Urban VIII to issue in 1624 a Papal Bull threatening excommunication to anyone who profaned the churches by taking tobacco within them. In Italy, however, there was never any general edict against the use of tobacco in its proper place, as was the case in so many other countries.

One bit of the history of smoking in Italy may be interesting to members of the American Expeditionary Force and to others who have had some personal experience with the kind of tobacco usually obtainable in European countries where the tobacco industry is under governmental control. Early in the seventeenth century it became evident to many monarchs that they could materially increase the incomes of their states by imposing import duties on tobacco. In Italy the Duke of Mantua evolved what appeared to be an even better scheme; he forbade the importation of tobacco by anyone except the one person to whom the monopoly of importing and selling both spirits and tobacco had been granted for a flat—and fat—yearly rental. Many other European nations later instituted similar arrangements for governmental monopolies of tobacco, as the plan was quickly found to be—as it still is—a most successful one from the standpoint of raising revenues, although it is doubtful whether it raises the quality of tobacco available for smokers in those particular countries.

〄〄

The story of the introduction of smoking into central and northern Europe is rather confused, largely because of the means by which the habit was spread throughout that region. In Italy, Spain, Portugal and France, the tobacco plant was grown and esteemed as a medicine by 1565 at the latest, and shortly thereafter it had also reached the Netherlands and Germany and Austria, but not for smoking purposes; up to that time the only European smokers were the Spanish, Portuguese and French settlers in the New World. Very soon after the habit reached England in 1565, it had been adopted by the other European maritime nations, and the stage was set for the introduction of the custom into the interior of Europe.

Although merchants from England appear to have started smoking in Hamburg shortly before 1600, and although a book published in Frankfort in 1616 contains a picture of a German using a pipe similar to the earliest

English clay, the principal cause of the diffusion of the habit of smoking throughout central Europe was the Thirty Years War. That religious and political battle-royal, which used Germany as its principal arena, involved almost every European nation sometime between 1618 and 1648. Soldiers from England, Spain, Holland, Italy, Denmark, Sweden, Norway and Switzerland, as well as from the various parts of Germany and Austria, such as Prussia, Saxony, Bavaria and Bohemia, stormed up and down the battle ground for a generation, alternately fighting and plundering the countryside for their sustenance. At the beginning of the conflict some of the combatants were smokers—such as the French, English, Spanish, Dutch and Italians—and some were non-smokers. By the end of the war all of the participants had not only learned the habit but had also inaugurated the use of tobacco in every country in which they had fought, through which they had marched, or on which they lived between campaigns.

In Saxony, for instance, the people first saw pipes in use by the English soldiers whom Count Grey had brought to the assistance of the King of Bohemia in 1620. The Spanish soldiers under General Spinola started the custom among the inhabitants of the Palatinate a few years later. In some districts even the women had taken up smoking by 1642. Although there are only these few details about the way the central European countries began to smoke, it is evident that the English were primarily responsible for the introduction of the habit in Germany. The Low German "smoken" is an important indication of the English influence, as is the bowl of the typical German pipe, which is obviously patterned after the bowl of the long English clay pipe.

63

It was also the Thirty Years War that made tobacco-smoking a common practice in Sweden. Norway had become acquainted with tobacco in 1616, and the people along the Scandinavian coasts had learned to smoke late in the sixteenth or early in the seventeenth centuries from the English and Dutch sailors who reached their shores, but the habit had not penetrated into the inland of Sweden. Then Gustavus Adolphus, ruler of Sweden, led his forces into Germany to take part in the Thirty Years War; smoking soon became as popular with his troops as it did with the various armies during the World War, and on their return home the Swedish soldiers quickly spread the habit throughout their country.

The natives of Australia and New Zealand did not take up smoking until the eighteenth century. For some unknown reason they did not learn the habit from their neighbors in Malaysia and Polynesia, who had had some contacts with the Australians and New Zealanders for many centuries and who had become smokers shortly after 1600. None of the first white explorers to reach either island found any evidence of smoking by the aborigines, and it was not until the English finally settled in Australia in 1787 and New Zealand in 1814 that the British colonists introduced the habit to the islanders.

The Conquistadores

8

WHILE THE PORTUGUESE mariners and merchants were extending their power and prestige eastward around the Cape of Good Hope, evincing little or no interest in the Western Hemisphere except in Brazil, the Spaniards were busily engaged in conquering and colonizing extensive areas of North America, Central America, the West Indies, and South America. Since the natives of most of the regions which thus fell under the domination of the Spaniards were smokers long before the arrival of the first Europeans, this part of the story of tobacco concerns only a few of the many countries that became Spanish possessions. Tobacco-smoking antedated the arrival of the Spaniards in all of their settlements in the New World except Argentina and Paraguay, and Peru and Chile.

Shortly after Cortez had conquered Mexico, efforts were made by the Spaniards to colonize Argentina, which had been discovered by Juan de Solis in 1516. The first white settlement (later abandoned) in that region was founded in 1527 by Sebastian Cabot, who had left the employ of England and had entered the service of Spain, on whose behalf he undertook a voyage to establish definitely the position of the meridian line which had been laid down in the Treaty of Tordesillas as the boundary between the Spanish and the Portuguese spheres of colonization; on reaching the Rio de la Plata, however, Cabot became so interested in the potential resources of Argentina that he abandoned his survey in favor of developing the new country. Eight years later the Spaniards built at Asunción, in Paraguay, their first permanent settlement in South America and also made the first of their three attempts to establish a colony at Buenos Aires. In the third quarter of the sixteenth century various Spanish towns were built in the interior, to which the settlers brought from Spain cattle and horses that became the ancestors of those for which the pampas are now so famous.

In the meantime, the Spaniards were extending their conquests southward from Mexico along the Pacific coast of South America. Pizarro landed in Peru in 1531 and founded Lima, its present capital, in 1535, in which year Chile was also invaded by the conquistadores. The Spaniards had great difficulty in asserting their dominion over the latter country; although Santiago was founded by Pedro de Valdiva in 1541, most of the next century was spent in constant warfare between the conquerors and the rebellious natives, and it was not until 1640 that a lasting peace was finally effected.

In Argentina, Paraguay, Peru and Chile, the Spaniards introduced smoking, and there, as proof of the Spanish influence, the natives still prefer the cigar and cigarette to the pipe. It is interesting to note that in one part of this territory, in the range of the Andes along the western coast, the natives have not yet taken to smoking, but generally

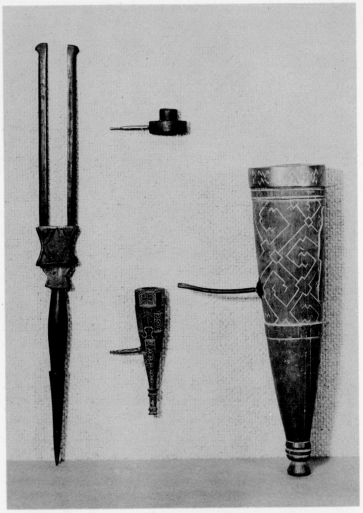

SMOKING EQUIPMENT FROM SOUTH AMERICA

*The Colombian cigar-holder is set upright in the ground, with
a very large cigar wedged between the tines. The larger of the
conical wooden Peruvian pipes weighs over three pounds. The
small pipe is from Patagonia.*

chew or lick tobacco instead. In this region the practice of chewing tobacco probably owes its popularity to the much older custom of chewing the leaves of the coca plant—which, by the way, should not be confused with the shrub from whose seeds we get our harmless beverage; coca leaves, from which cocaine is obtained, apparently have been used as a narcotic by the Indians of the Andes since long before the discovery of America. Licking tobacco is a custom unique to this general area; the Indians boil down the tobacco leaves with water until they have a thick black syrup, small quantities of which they occasionally lick up—a method of taking tobacco which, happily, seems to have little or no chance of becoming generally popular.

The first European to reach the Philippine Islands was a Portuguese, Francisco Serrão, who, shipwrecked while acting as second-in-command of a Portuguese expedition engaged in exploring the Malay Archipelago in 1511, succeeded in making his way in a native boat to Mindanao, one of the Philippines. Ten years later, one of his countrymen, Ferdinand Magellan, arrived at the islands on his famous voyage, only to meet his death at the hands of the natives. As Magellan had been employed by Spain in an effort to prove that certain islands of the East Indies lay within the Spanish sphere of influence as determined by the Treaty of Tordesillas, he had claimed the islands for his patrons. For some years thereafter there was an active dispute over the rival claims of Portugal and Spain to the Philippines, which Spain finally won. After the founding of Manila in 1571, active colonization was conducted, largely by Spanish soldiers and missionaries from Mexico.

Along with other attributes of civilization, the Spanish settlers brought to the natives first the custom of smoking and then the tobacco plant. Evidently both the habit and the plant were introduced, at the latest, shortly after the founding of Manila. Even today the Filipinos are one of the relatively few eastern peoples who follow to a large extent the Spanish and Mexican custom of smoking cigars; while they also use pipes, they frequently practice both methods simultaneously, for they insert rolled tobacco leaves into the pipe bowl, thus converting the pipe into a sort of right-angled cigar-holder.

The Far North

9

ALTHOUGH the Alaskan Eskimos were not the last
people to learn about smoking, it seems fitting to
make the account of their acquisition of the habit
the last chapter of the story of tobacco's travels around the
world.

The Eskimos east of Alaska and the Yukon territory
became acquainted with tobacco either from the North
American Indians or from the English and the Danes who
settled among them; for example, some of the eastern
Eskimo pipes are modeled after those of the Indians who
once inhabited so much of the northeastern part of the
present-day United States, while others are copied from English and Danish pipes, and in Greenland the Eskimo word
for tobacco is obviously of Danish origin. In Alaska, however, the introduction of smoking is quite a different story.

Some of the Eskimos inhabiting the southern part of
Alaska did not learn to smoke until after 1833, when the
practice was brought to them by the Russians who established settlements in that locality. However, when the early

explorers—Captain Cook in 1778, and others in 1816 and 1826—first visited various parts of northwestern Alaska they found that the Eskimos there were already familiar with the use of tobacco. This habit they could not have learned from the American Indians, for the contacts between those Eskimos and the Indians were very slight. Hence the only people who could have taught the natives of northwestern Alaska to smoke were their neighbors on the other side of the Bering Strait, with whom they had traded and fought for many years.

This deduction is confirmed by factual evidence. In the first place, there is the kind of pipe used by those Eskimo tribes which had begun to smoke prior to their contacts with the Russians or Europeans. Their pipe generally consists of a curved wooden stem on the concave side of which is placed a metal bowl of very small bore and with a projecting flange on the upper end. This peculiar shape is found in only one other locality—the northeastern part of Siberia, where the Chukchees and some of the adjacaent tribes use a pipe of almost identical form. Both the Chukchees and the Alaskan Eskimos, moreover, have identical expedients for overcoming the difficulties of driving a bore with their primitive tools in the curved stem. So similar are these pipes on both sides of the Bering Strait that even an expert hesitates to identify a given specimen as being Alaskan or Asian.

Secondly, there is the unusual method of smoking practised by the Alaskan Eskimos and the Chukchees. Both races place reindeer hair in the bottom of the bowl in order to prevent the tobacco from being drawn into the stem and then fill the bowl with a mixture of finely chopped tobacco and wood. The smoker completely exhausts the contents of

70

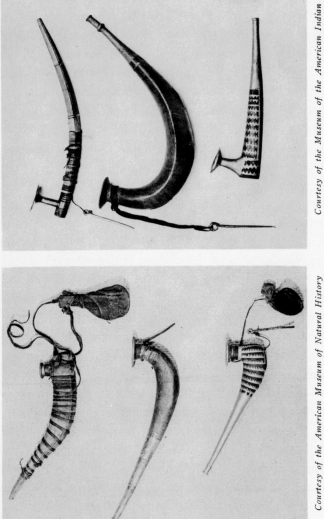

PIPES FROM SIBERIA AND ALASKA

The close similarity between the pipes of Northeastern Asia, shown at the left, and those of Alaska, shown at the right, is readily apparent.

his pipe in a few deep pulls, drawing the smoke so far into his lungs as to sometimes bring on a state very near that of intoxication.

Final corroboration of the Asiatic source of Alaskan smoking is found in the Eskimo word for the sort of pipe described above. While Eskimos call the ordinary white man's pipe, with which they of course have become familiar, by a name closely resembling the English "pipe," the other, and older, form of Eskimo pipe is called "kuinya." This word appears in the vocabularies of many of the different Alaskan Eskimo groups, but it cannot be connected with any of their stem-words, from which so much of their language is derived. On the other hand, "kuinya" very closely resembles the sound of the Chukchees' word for pipe, which, as we should write it, is "koiñiñ."

When tobacco thus crossed from Asia to Alaska, it had made a complete eastward circuit around the globe. The route by which it eventually reached the Eskimos is clearly defined. The Portuguese had learned to smoke at their colonies in Brazil. Later their voyages to the East brought Portuguese explorers to Japan, where they introduced the use of tobacco. Japanese invaders took the custom to Korea, whence it spread to Manchuria. The Manchurian merchants propagated the practise throughout Asia, until finally it reached the tribes living in the north-eastern tip of the continent. When these Chukchees crossed the Bering Strait, either for commerce or for war, they taught the Alaskan Eskimos how to smoke. In this manner the custom of smoking had traveled from South America to Europe, from Europe to Asia, and thence back again to the northern tip of the hemisphere which was its original home.

Forms and Fashions

10

ONCE TOBACCO had made its way to all parts of the globe, its popularity increased rapidly and steadily, and new recruits joined the great army of smokers daily. When the early royal interdictions proved to be unavailing, most sovereigns gave up the unequal struggle against tobacco and instead gloated over the substantial revenues which its use brought to their coffers, either from taxes or from state monopolies. To be sure, the herb continued to encounter occasional opposition, for even as late as the twentieth century such crusaders as Carrie Nation and Billy Sunday anathematized it, but the principal changes in the world's tobacco habits since 1650 have been merely those of form and fashion.

The history of smoking in England offers one of the best examples of the shifting fashions in the use of tobacco. After Hawkins and his companions had taught their fellow-countrymen the pleasures of the pipe, and particularly after Raleigh's influence had persuaded the quality to take up smoking, the new habit gained many followers throughout the length and breadth of England; despite the fact that in those early days tobacco was sold—generally at apothecaries' shops—for its weight in silver, rich and poor alike soon became ardent smokers. It was not long before the ability "to drink tobacco with a grace" was considered a necessary accomplishment for every man of fashion, and the dandy frequently spent hours being tutored in the "sleights" of tobacco so that he could exhale the smoke through his nostrils, blow rings, and do other smoker's tricks. As the swell smoked at all times and all places, in the theatre as well as on the street, he carried with him a complete kit of smokers' accessories—a tobacco box, a pair of tongs for lighting his pipe with a burning coal, and a tobacco stopper for pressing the dried leaves firmly into his pipe bowl, all elaborately wrought in expensive materials. His pipe, however, was the same sort of clay pipe smoked, usually turn and turn about around the table, by his inferiors, except in the relatively rare cases where the poor man made shift with a walnut shell and a straw or where milord sported a pipe of silver. So great was the demand for pipes that in 1619—only fifteen years after his philippic against tobacco—James I condescended to grant a royal charter to the Society of Tobacco-pipe-makers; the guild's motto, faintly reminiscent of the pipe-philosophy of the first Bushongo smoker, was "Let brotherly love continue."

For almost one hundred and fifty years after the introduction of smoking into England, there were few important changes of either fashion or form in the tobacco habits of the nation. As the cost of tobacco gradually decreased, the number of smokers grew, until finally all the English of both sexes and of all ages and classes were confirmed smokers. When the Great Plague ravaged London in 1665, the belief that tobacco guarded one against contagion led to the rather astounding result that school children were actually compelled to smoke in their class rooms and were soundly whipped for the failure to do so. But until almost 1700 the smoking customs of the country remained the same, except that as pipes became less expensive they were no longer circulated among a company of smokers, and smoking equipment underwent only one minor alteration, which was the introduction of the longer and larger-bowled pipe then in use in Holland. The Dutch had early learned the art of pipe-making from the English, whose very words for the tools of the trade were used in Holland for many years thereafter, and most of the seventeenth-century English pipes were made in Holland of English clay. As the Dutch had become incessant smokers very shortly after they had first become acquainted with tobacco, they were not satisfied with such small bowls as the English used. They evolved a larger clay pipe, with a greater tobacco capacity and with a long, gracefully curved stem tipped with glaze to prevent its sticking to the smoker's lips. When the Dutch William II ascended the throne of England with Mary his wife in 1689, he brought the longer Dutch pipes, known as "aldermen" across the Channel, where they came into great favor among the gentry. Of necessity, the working man had to keep to the handier and older English form with a stem about eight inches long, and the Irish and Scotch, possibly merely through innate obstinacy, clung to their even shorter "dudeens" and "cutties."

In the opening years of the eighteenth century, smoking had reached its zenith in England, being a more universal habit among the British than it is even today, only to suffer a sudden and sharp decrease in popularity in fashionable circles. The clergy, the students, the country squires, the merchants, and the people of the lower classes puffed away at their pipes as constantly as ever, but Society, with a capital S, began to regard the practice with disfavor. Their change in attitude apparently was caused by the very popularity of smoking, for a pipe was no longer, as it at first had been, the mark of the swell, but was seen in the mouth of the commonest laborer. The beaux, wanting a new fad to set them apart from their inferiors, found one that enabled them— and their ladies—to continue to indulge in tobacco when they adopted from the French court the use of snuff, which had long been a fashionable practice in Paris. Beau Nash interpreted the new trend correctly when he forbade smoking in the public rooms at Bath, and soon the pipe was ostracized from polite society. In the upper strata of society, taking snuff soon became as habitual as smoking is now, and the swells discarded their smoking paraphernalia for equally elaborate snuff-boxes of gold, silver and porcelain. When one dandy was complimented on his dainty Sèvres snuff-box, he replied modestly, "Yes, it is a nice summer box—but certainly would be inappropriate for winter wear." With such disdain did the best people come to regard tobacco that Dr. Johnson may have thought that he was sounding the death-knell of the pipe when he said in 1773, "smoking has gone out".

But smoking in England continued to be popular among persons not amenable to the dictates of fashion, even though it remained under a social ban until well into the nineteenth century. Although snuff was still favored by the upper crust when Victoria became queen in 1837, it was just about that time that the renaissance of smoking began, thanks largely to the cigar. The cigar, which had been common in the Americas for several centuries and in Spain since the early days of tobacco in Europe, had apparently failed to win many followers elsewhere until the end of the eighteenth century. Although it was sufficiently well known in Germany in 1796 so that the first cigar factory in Northern Europe was established at Hamburg in that year, this form of smoking did not become a factor in the tobacco history of England until after the Peninsula War. The British officers who fought against Napoleon's forces in Spain and Portugal in 1808-1814 took to cigars during that campaign and were later responsible for their introduction into England; their approbation did much to make the innovation fashionable as soon as Great Britain reduced the high import duties on cigars to more reasonable figures. Although at first cigars were obtainable only from the captains of the West Indian ships docking at Liverpool, Bristol and London, in 1830 a quarter of a million pounds of them were imported into England, and it is estimated that by 1860 fully half of the urban consumption of tobacco in England was in the form of cigars. The new kind of smoking endeared itself to the man of fashion for three reasons: it was novel, it was daintier than a pipe, and it was sufficiently expensive so that it remained for some time a rich man's luxury.

The resultant revival of fashionable smoking at first had, however, one marked difference from the earlier days when pipes had been in favor among the aristocracy, for the Victorian swells smoked privately rather than publicly. The fumes of tobacco were thought to be distasteful to feminine nostrils (Queen Victoria detested smoking), so the nine-teenth century gentleman was accustomed to retire to a special smoking room where, donning a cap and smoking jacket to protect his hair and clothes from the taint of tobacco, he puffed away at his cigar in masculine comfort until such time as he wished to return to the company of the ladies. The unfortunate whose house did not boast a smoking room was either banished to the stables or back halls when he wished to smoke or else had recourse to the uncomfortable alterna-tive of smoking secretly by his bedroom fireplace, blowing surreptitious clouds of smoke up the chimney so that no telltale odor would remain.

Later another war changed the tobacco habits of England by the introduction of a third form of smoking—the cigar-ette. Many British military and naval officers engaged in the Crimean War in 1854-1856 had adopted this way of smoking tobacco, which was fairly common in Russia, Turkey and the Levant. On their return to England, the heroes were aped by swells and "snobs" alike, and the cigarettes they smoked (as well as the beards they wore) were soon everywhere in evidence. But cigarettes, unlike cigars, were within the reach of even the shortest purses, so by about 1870 the latest vogue in smoking had reached all classes.

Until about the middle of the nineteenth century, the pipes smoked in England, save in a few rare instances, had been clays. First the Elizabethan clays, then the "aldermen" which William II introduced about 1700, and after 1815 the even longer "churchwardens" had been the correct pipes for gentlemen, while throughout the entire period the humbler classes had used the shorter clay pipes. There had been, it is

77

true, a few pipes made of other materials, including silver and iron, but the only form to become a serious rival of the clay prior to 1850 was the meerschaum.

It was in 1723 that an Austrian count decided to have a pipe bowl fashioned from a lump of meerschaum which he had been given while on a visit to Turkey. The work was entrusted to a shoemaker who, as a side-line, carved pipes for wealthy smokers. From the piece of "Foam of the Sea" he cut two pipes, one for his patron and one for himself. Noticing as he smoked his pipe that the bowl took on a clear brown color wherever it touched his hands, which were naturally waxy from his trade, the cobbler experimented by waxing the entire bowl, which then not only assumed a beautiful, even, brown tint—the goal of every subsequent possessor of a meerschaum pipe—but also smoked much sweeter than before. Meerschaum pipes soon became great favorites among gentlemen and connoisseurs, but in England they supplemented, and did not displace, the time-honored clays.

During the rest of its long reign, the clay pipe underwent one further change, when it became the custom to enrich the bowls with fanciful designs. Such pipes, while fairly popular in England, were mostly of French manufacture. The bowls took on a myriad of different forms, such as carrots, skulls, dogs' heads, steins and the like, and, at a later date, even a railway locomotive, which of course appeared particularly realistic when puffs of tobacco smoke came out the engine's smokestack. The heights of contemporary fame were reached when a man became prominent enough to have his head modelled—or possibly caricatured—on a pipe bowl; thus honored were Louis Napoleon,

Victor Hugo and, despite his strong aversion to tobacco, the Duke of Wellington.

For some years it had been obvious that wood, of the proper kind, would be the ideal material for pipe bowls. Clay, porcelain and meerschaum were too fragile; metals were too heavy and became too hot when smoked. Cherry and willow wood were tried, but without much success. An early approach to a satisfactory wood was the root of the dwarf-oak growing in the Black Forest of Germany, which the peasants had long delighted to carve into elaborate pipe bowls, but the ideal was not discovered until about 1850, when the root of the tree-heath, or bruyère, was first employed in the manufacture of pipes. The story runs that a French pipe-maker, on a pilgrimage to Corsica to pay homage to the memory of Napoleon, broke or lost his own pipe and commissioned a Corsican peasant to make him another; at the first puff the Frenchman might well have cried "Eureka!" for he had discovered the long-awaited perfect wood for pipes. He took home with him some of the native root from which the peasant had fashioned the bowl and turned out several pipes in his own shop, thereby introducing to the smoking world what is now known as the briar pipe, for the French "bruyère" was corrupted first into "bruyer", then "brier" and later "briar." The new pipe was introduced into England, where it speedily drove out—as it did elsewhere—the old clays, and proved such a satisfactory pipe that its use became universal. Fortunately for the pipe-smoker, the cultivation of the tree-heath is not confined to Corsica alone; it is grown in many places on the Mediterranean in sufficient quantity to supply the present world-wide demand for briar pipes.

The importance of the discovery of the briar pipe and of the greatly increased use of the cigarette can hardly be over-emphasized. While it is true that the various nations still use, to a very large extent, their own original forms of pipes, some of which have been described and pictured in the preceding pages, short wooden pipes and cigarettes are now as ubiquitous as European clothes and American automobiles. The cigarette and the briar pipe have put tobacco within the reach of every man's pocketbook and have provided him with two convenient forms of smoking by which tobacco has come to be the smoker's constant companion, ever ready to heighten his moments of pleasure, to solace him in times of distress, and to lend a soothing influence on those all too frequent occasions when he must wrestle with the multitudinous problems which latterly seem to have become our daily lot.

Appendix

If, in an attempt to learn something about the contents of your cigar, cigarette, or pipe-smoking mixture, you should look up "Tobacco" in a dictionary, you would find some such statement as this:

> "Tobacco—Any solanaceous plant of the genus Nicotiana, especially of the various species cultivated for their leaves, the most common being *N. tabacum,* of South American origin, but no longer known in the wild state. It is a tall annual with ample ovate or lanceolate leaves and white or pink tubular flowers."

Since that would hardly satisfy your thirst for tobacco knowledge, you might go further and turn to "Solanaceae," only to find this:

> "A family of strong-scented, often narcotic, herbs, shrubs or trees (order Polemoniales), comprising about 75 genera and 1800 species, of wide distribution; the nightshade family. They have alternate leaves and often showy flowers . . ."

Long before you had read far enough to learn that botanists have put tobacco on the same family tree as the tomato, the red pepper, the potato, and the deadly nightshade—from

81

the layman's point of view, a most strange group of relatives —you would have decided to look elsewhere for a more realistic description of what you smoke. In your search you might run across a very scientific treatise and be further confounded and confused to learn, from a chemist's analysis, that tobacco contains nicotine, resinous fats, malic, citric, pectic and oxalic acids, cellulose, albuminoids, and ash—only the first and last of which you had ever associated with your idea of smoking. At that point you might stop wondering about *what* you smoke and begin instead to worry *why* you smoke anything that can be described by such unsavoury scientific terms.

Unfortunately, it is difficult for the layman to find an easily comprehended description of tobacco in general or of the various types of tobacco that are in ordinary commercial use. The following pages contain information of that sort which I hope may be of interest to the average smoker.

Scientifically speaking, tobacco is a narcotic, and the nicotine which it contains has been used with lethal effect on dogs and cats and rabbits—but so has a poison easily derived from tobacco's poor relation, the potato. Tobacco is cultivated almost all over the world in the temperate and tropical zones, ranging from Quebec and Stockholm in the North to Chile and the Cape of Good Hope in the South. Its straight stem, which may be from three to fifteen feet high, glossy green leaves and showy flowers combine to make it a plant of great beauty. Although there are between forty and fifty different varieties of tobacco, all of which are indigenous to the Western Hemisphere, the only ones of any importance commercially are the following:

Nicotiana tabacum. This, the tallest of all varieties, supplies the bulk of the tobacco grown and used throughout the world. A native of South and Central America, it was first brought to North America when John Rolfe imported it from Trinidad into Virginia about 1612. Except for the few types mentioned under the two other botanical varieties of the plant described below, all of the tobaccos discussed hereafter come from this single variety.

Nicotiana rustica. A native of Mexico, this variety is now cultivated chiefly in Europe, Asia, and Africa, supplying the Turkish, Latakia, Sumatra and Java tobaccos mentioned later. It grows to a height of only three or four feet.

Nicotiana persica. This strain, the smallest of the three varieties, is grown only in Persia, where it produces Shiraz tobacco.

From a practical, not a botanical, standpoint, the various types of tobacco produced throughout the world may be divided into two main groups, the Manufacturing Types, used for cigarettes, pipe-smoking mixtures, chewing tobacco and snuff, and the Cigar Types, used primarily for making of cigars.

In considering the Manufacturing Types, particularly those grown in the United States, it is convenient to make a further division of tobaccos into air-cured (both light and dark), fire-cured and flue-cured. These various curing processes, which are conducted by the tobacco farmers before they market their crops, involve nothing more than a drying of the tobacco leaf. The different methods are just what their names imply: in air-curing, no artificial heat is used; in fire-curing, open fires are burned in the drying sheds; in flue-curing, metal flues conduct the heat through the barns

83

without admitting the smoke. As the fire-cured and dark air-cured tobaccos raised in this country are generally either exported or used domestically for chewing tobacco and snuff, they will not concern us any longer, and we shall confine our attention to the light air-cured and the flue-cured types.

The Cigar Types are also subdivided into three groups, according to the use to which they are put: filler, binder and wrapper. Roughly it may be said that a cigar is made by enclosing a handful of tobacco (the filler) in a single leaf (the binder), and by then carefully adding another single leaf (the wrapper) as the outside covering. Wrapper leaf is the very finest cigar tobacco, for not only is its flavor of great importance, but so also are its elasticity, texture and appearance. Tobacco grown for wrappers is, when unsatisfactory, used as binders, just as second-grade binder leaves are used as fillers. All of the Cigar Types are air-cured.

The following discussion of the most important kinds of tobacco is concerned with the leaves after they have been cured, since the growing leaves do not show the wide variations in color and other characteristics apparent after curing.

VIRGINIAN

Our largest tobacco crop is generally spoken of either as "Virginian" or as "Bright" tobacco. The latter name describes its appearance well, for its lemon to orange color is the lightest of any of the usual domestic varieties; the former title is something of a misnomer, since both North and South Carolina produce more of this leaf than Virginia does, and very large quantities are also grown in Georgia and Florida.

The flavor of this flue-cured tobacco is even more distinctive than its color; that it tastes rather sweet is not strange, for chemical analysis shows that it has a high natural sugar content. Virginian tobacco is much used domestically in pipe tobaccos and in both straight and blended cigarettes, as well as being exported to many foreign countries; in Great Britain, for instance, where this tobacco has been popular since it was first raised by the English colonists at Jamestown, Virginian leaf accounts for about 98% of the tobacco bought from the United States and for about 80% of all the tobacco imports.

BURLEY

Burley tobacco is a distinctive variety which was first produced in 1864, since which time it has grown to be the second largest tobacco crop of the United States. It is produced mainly in Tennessee, Kentucky and southern Ohio. This air-cured leaf, which is low in nicotine content, is from yellow-green to yellow-brown in color, much of it being about the shade of the olive drab of army uniforms. As it is rather mild in flavor and has the property of absorbing a remarkable quantity of the flavoring sauces which are usually added to smoking mixtures, it is an important constituent in domestic pipe tobaccos and blended cigarettes.

MARYLAND

From the standpoint of the tobacco manufacturer, Maryland tobacco, one of the smaller crops, is of special value because it has the best capacity of any domestic type for holding fire. Since its aroma is neutral, it may safely be added in order to improve the "burn" of a blend without disturbing the taste or flavor of the other constituents. Maryland leaf is thin and dry, and of a dark brown color. It is grown in southern Maryland between the Potomac River and Chesapeake Bay, and, like Burley, is one of the light air-cured types.

PERIQUE

The smallest, yet at the same time one of the most important, United States tobacco crops is Perique, which is grown only in St. James Parish, Louisiana. It is not a distinct variety of the plant; the peculiar properties which Perique possesses are entirely the result of the unusual method of curing the leaf, which over a period of time is alternately pressed and then allowed, without pressure, to soak in its own juices. The resultant tobacco is very strong, yet pleasant in taste, and almost jet black. While it is used for chewing, snuffing and straight smoking, Perique has an unusually fragrant aroma which makes it a particularly desirable component in pipe-tobacco mixtures.

TURKISH

Even a brief description of Turkish tobacco should properly be introduced by mentioning a few relevant matters that do not seem to be generally understood. In the first place, it is regretful but true that a considerable quantity of Chinese tobacco masquerades as Turkish in the cheaper brands of cigarettes and pipe-smoking mixtures. Secondly, Egyptian cigarettes contain no Egyptian tobacco, the better varieties being made of the Turkish leaf; no tobacco is grown in Egypt, its cultivation there having been forbidden many years ago because of its harmful effect on the already weak soil. Lastly, most of the Turkish tobacco imported to this country is actually produced in Greece, which is quite as it should be, for the former Turkish territory of Macedonia, now Greek, raises the very finest of this type of tobacco.

The leaves of Turkish tobacco are small, ranging from about three to ten inches in length, as compared with lengths of from one to one and a half feet for many United States tobaccos. The color is light, from light brown to light yellow. All Turkish leaf is air-cured. Turkish tobacco has a special aroma that makes it particularly pleasant in cigarette blends and places it in the rank with Latakia and Shiraz as the finest of pipe tobaccos. There are many different varieties, of which the finest come from the Macedonian, Smyrna and Samsoun districts.

Of the large production in Macedonia, the very best crop is the Xanthi tobacco, an egg-shaped leaf of fine texture and of orange to reddish brown color. It burns well, has a high nicotine content, is very aromatic and has a fresh, sweet taste that makes it popular in blends for cigarettes and pipe tobacco.

The pale yellow Smyrna tobacco, which is so fine as to be almost silky, is the most aromatic of all Turkish varieties, so that it is sometimes said that no good cigarette can be made unless it contains some Smyrna leaf. It is second in quality to the Xanthi crop, however, because it has a poor "burn." Its nicotine content is low.

Like Xanthi tobacco, that produced in the region of Samsoun has a good "burn" and a high nicotine content, but it is less aromatic than the other two types described. Its lance-shaped leaves are delicate in texture and are from reddish brown to reddish yellow in color.

87

LATAKIA

Latakia, a small plant which grows to a height of only about three feet, is cultivated in northern Syria. In the preparation of this tobacco, the entire plant above ground—even the flowers—is cured over open fires, which possibly explains why Latakia's pleasant flavor is described sometimes as resembling "ashes of roses" and sometimes as being like the aroma from a wood fire. Latakia tobacco is thin, dark brown, and low in nicotine content. As it ranks among the very best tobaccos, it is considered an essential element in most of the high-grade smoking mixtures.

PERSIAN

The tobacco grown in Persia is one of the few important distinct species of the plant, being Nicotiana persica. It is very strong in nicotine. The famous Persian variety known as Shiraz is generally considered to be one of the finest tobaccos grown, particularly for the pipe. The light yellow leaves have a mild flavor quite similar to Turkish and Latakia tobaccos. Its one disadvantage is that it does not burn well, but in the East this difficulty is overcome by placing a glowing piece of charcoal on top of the tobacco in the bowl of the water pipe. Shiraz tobacco deserves mention here only because of its excellent quality; as a practical matter the average smoker is not apt to experience the delight of smoking it, since it is but little used commercially outside of its native land.

CUBAN

Tobacco grown in Cuba, frequently referred to as Havana tobacco, has long been acclaimed as the world's best cigar tobacco, but not all Cuban tobaccos merit that praise. The choicest leaves are grown in the Vuelta Abajo, Partidos and Remedios districts. So fine are those produced in some few parts of the Vuelta Abajo region that the cigars into which they are made are hoarded like great vintage wines, to be brought forth only on very special occasions. Straight Havana cigars—that is, those containing only Cuban tobacco—are generally made from leaves from the Vuelta Abajo and Partidos districts, the Partidos region being particularly famous for the light and glossy wrapper which it produces. Remedios tobacco has a higher flavor and heavier body than the other two types mentioned, making it particularly suitable for blending with United States cigar tobaccos.

Generally speaking, Cuban tobacco has a high nicotine content, a rich flavor and a peculiar aroma. The leaf is apt to be small and is of a rich brown color.

SUMATRA

Sumatra tobacco is ideal for cigar wrappers, and Sumatra leaf imported to the United States is used exclusively for that purpose. It is glossy, it has a good color and it is remarkably elastic—three vitally important qualifications for wrapper tobacco. Its flavor is rather neutral, and it may therefore be used with almost any kind of filler leaf.

JAVA

Java produces a tobacco that is tough and has a heavy body. Although it is somewhat similar to Sumatra tobacco, only a very small part of the crop is suitable for wrapper leaves. Wrapper leaves alone are exported from Java to the United States, but in other countries Java tobacco of the lower grades is used for cigar binders and fillers.

UNITED STATES CIGAR TOBACCOS

In the United States the Cigar Type makes up a little less than a tenth of the entire production of tobacco, but some of it, notably that grown for wrappers, is of very high quality. The chief centers of cigar tobacco cultivation are in the valley of the Connecticut River in Connecticut and Massachusetts, in northern Florida and Southern Georgia, sections of Pennsylvania and New York, in parts of Wisconsin and Minnesota, and in the Miami valley in Ohio.

Practically all of the domestic wrapper tobacco is raised under shade in the sandy soils of the Connecticut Valley, where the first cigar tobacco cultivation in the United States was started about 1825. The practice of providing artificial shade by covering and enclosing the fields in cheesecloth, which was inaugurated in 1906, not only shields the plants from the direct rays of the sun, but also equalizes the temperature and conserves the moisture. The leaves are raised from either Havana or Sumatra seeds and are particularly well suited for wrappers, being large and strong, yet elastic, of fine texture and light color. The prime leaves are considered by some to be superior to the imported Sumatra wrapper leaves in taste, but somewhat inferior in elasticity and covering qualities. Since only the best leaves are used for wrappers, this region also supplies a great deal of binder tobacco. Quite similar tobacco is produced in the Georgia-Florida district.

The next best cigar tobacco raised in this country comes from scattered areas in Wisconsin and Minnesota, where the entire production is used for binders.

In the neighborhood of Lancaster, Pennsylvania, and in the northern Pennsylvania and southern New York district centering around Elmira, the tobacco crop resembles that of the Connecticut Valley in appearance, but most of it is used as filler tobacco.

In Ohio nothing but filler tobacco is grown, for use primarily in stogies, cheroots and the cheaper brands of cigars. Here there are two important types: Zimmer Spanish, which resembles fairly closely the imported Cuban tobacco, and Little Dutch, which is popular not only as a cigar leaf but also in pipe smoking mixtures.

Bibliography

Innumerable books, pamphlets and articles have been written about tobacco and smoking. To those listed below I would direct the attention of any reader who may wish to inquire further into tobacco's fascinating history.

APPERSON, G. L.—*"The Social History of Smoking"*, G. P. Putnam's Sons, 1916.

BILLINGS, E. R.—*"Tobacco, Its History, Varieties, Culture, Manufacture, and Commerce"*, American Publishing Co., 1875.

BRENNAN, W. A.—*"Tobacco Leaves"*, The Collegiate Press, 1915.

COMES, ORAZIO—*"Histoire, Géographie et Statistique du Tabac"*, Naples, 1900.

DUNHILL, ALFRED—*"The Pipe Book"*, The MacMillan Co., 1924.

FAIRHOLT, F. W.—*"Tobacco: Its History and Associations"*, Chatto and Windus, London, 1876.

FIELD MUSEUM OF NATURAL HISTORY, *Anthropology Leaflets Nos. 15, 16, 17, 18, 19, and 29.*

GOODRICH, L. CARRINGTON—*"Early Prohibitions of Tobacco in China and Manchuria"*, in Journal of American Oriental Society, 1938, Vol. 58.

HAMILTON, A. E.—*"This Smoking World"*, The Century Co., 1927.

LAIDLER, P. W.—*"Pipes and Smoking in South Africa"*, in Transactions of the Royal Society of South Africa, 1938, Vol. 26.

McGuire, Joseph D.—*"Pipes and Smoking Customs of the American Aborigines"*, in United States National Museum Report, 1897.

Murdoch, John—*"On the Siberian Origin of Some Customs of Western Eskimos"*, in American Anthropologist, Vol. 1.

Partington, Wilfred—*"Smoke Rings and Roundelays"*, Dodd, Mead & Co., 1925.

Penn, W. A.—*"The Soverane Herbe"*, E. P. Dutton & Co., 1901.

Pritchett, R. T.—*"Smokiana"*, Bernard Quartich, London, 1890.

Satow, Ernest M.—*"The Introduction of Tobacco to Japan"*, in Transactions of the Asiatic Society of Japan, 1878, Vol. 6.

Werner, Carl Avery—*"Tobaccoland"*, Tobacco Leaf Publishing Co., 1923.

West, George A.—*"Tobacco, Pipes and Smoking Customs of the American Indians"*, in Bulletin of the Public Museum of the City of Milwaukee, 1934, Vol. XVII.

Special mention should be made of the foremost bibliography of tobacco, entitled *"Tobacco: Its History Illustrated by the Books, Manuscripts and Engravings in the Library of George Arents, Jr."* and compiled by Jerome E. Brooks; for permission to print the solution of the mystery of Antonioto Baço, described in that catalogue, and for the courteous cooperation of the staffs of the museums from which I obtained some of the illustrations of this book, I wish to record my gratitude.

ARMS OF THE SOCIETY OF TOBACCO-PIPE-MAKERS
LONDON, ENGLAND, 1619

The Odyssey of Tobacco
with incidental decorative drawings
by Lois V. Schaeffer
has been designed, composed & printed
at the Sign of the Stone Book
in Hartford, Connecticut
for The Prospect Press.
The text has been set in
Linotype Granjon, with Corvinus Medium
and printed on ash-white Arak;
the photographs have been reproduced
in the collotype process.